Baltimore Orioles 2020

A Baseball Companion

Edited by R.J. Anderson, Craig Goldstein and Bret Sayre

Baseball Prospectus

Craig Brown, Steven Goldman and David Pease, Consultant Editors
Robert Au, Harry Pavlidis and Amy Pircher, Statistics Editors

Copyright © 2020 by DIY Baseball, LLC.
All rights reserved

This book or any part thereof may not be reproduced or transmitted in any form or by any means, electronic or mechanical, including photocopying, recording, or by any information storage and retrieval system, without permission in writing from the publisher.

Limit of Liability/Disclaimer of Warranty: While the publisher and the author have used their best efforts in preparing this book, they make no representations or warranties with respect to the accuracy or completeness of the contents of this book and specifically disclaim any implied warranties of merchantability or fitness for a particular purpose. No warranty may be created or extended by sales representatives or written sales materials. The advice and strategies contained herein may not be suitable for your situation. You should consult with a professional where appropriate. Neither the publisher nor the author shall be liable for any loss of profit or any other commercial damages, including but not limited to special, incidental, consequential, or other damages.

Library of Congress Cataloging-in-Publication Data:
paperback
ISBN-13: 978-1-949332-64-3

Project Credits
Cover Design: Michael Byzewski at Aesthetic Apparatus
Interior Design and Production: Jeff Pease, Dave Pease
Layout: Jeff Pease, Dave Pease

Baseball icon courtesy of Uberux, from https://www.shareicon.net/author/uberux

Ballpark diagram courtesy of Lou Spirito/THIRTY81 Project, https://thirty81project.com/

Manufactured in the United States of America
10 9 8 7 6 5 4 3 2 1

Table of Contents

Statistical Introduction v

Part 1: Team Analysis

Baltimore Orioles: Where Are You Going, Where Have You Been? 3
   Derek Albin, Jeffrey Paternostro and Matthew Trueblood

Performance Graphs 7

2019 Team Performance 8

2020 Team Projections 9

Team Personnel 10

Oriole Park at Camden Yards Stats 11

Orioles Team Analysis 13

Part 2: Player Analysis

Orioles Player Analysis 20

Orioles Prospects 117

Part 3: Featured Articles

The Baseball Is Juiced (Again) 133
   Robert Arthur

The Moral Hazard of Playing It Safe 137
   Craig Goldstein

Index of Names 143

Statistical Introduction

Sports are, fundamentally, a blend of athletic endeavor and storytelling. Baseball, like any other sport, tells its stories in so many ways: in the arc of a game from the stands or a season from the box scores, in photos, or even in numbers. At Baseball Prospectus, we understand that statistics don't replace observation or any of baseball's stories, but complement everything else that makes the game so much fun.

What stats help us with is with patterns and precision, variance and value. This book can help you learn things you may not see from watching a game or hundred, whether it's the path of a career over time or the breadth of the entire MLB. We'd also never ask you to choose between our numbers and the experience of viewing a game from the cheap seats or the comfort of your home; our publication combines running the numbers with observations and wisdom from some of the brightest minds we can find. But if you *do* want to learn more about the numbers beyond what's on the backs of player jerseys, let us help explain.

Offense

We've revised our methodology for determining batting value. Long-time readers of the book will notice that we've retired True Average in favor of a new metric: Deserved Runs Created Plus (DRC+). Developed by Jonathan Judge and our stats team, this statistic measures everything a player does at the plate–reaching base, hitting for power, making outs, and moving runners over–and puts it on a scale where 100 equals league-average performance. A DRC+ of 150 is terrific, a DRC+ of 100 is average and a DRC+ of 75 means you better be an excellent defender.

DRC+ also does a better job than any of our previous metrics in taking contextual factors into account. The model adjusts for how the park affects performance, but also for things like the talent of the opposing pitcher, value of different types of batted-ball events, league, temperature and other factors. It's able to describe a player's expected offensive contribution than any other statistic we've found over the years, and also does a better job of predicting future performance as well.

There's a lot more to DRC+'s story, and you can read all about it in greater depth near the end of this book.

Baltimore Orioles 2020

The other aspect of run-scoring is baserunning, which we quantify using Baserunning Runs. BRR not only records the value of stolen bases (or getting caught in the act), but also accounts for all the stuff that doesn't show up on the back of a baseball card: a runner's ability to go first to third on a single, or advance on a fly ball.

Defense

Where offensive value is *relatively* easy to identify and understand, defensive value is...not. Over the past dozen years, the sabermetric community has focused mostly on stats based on zone data: a real-live human person records the type of batted ball and estimated landing location, and models are created that give expected outs. From there, you can compare fielders' actual outs to those expected ones. Simple, right?

Unfortunately, zone data has two major issues. First, zone data is recorded by commercial data providers who keep the raw data private unless you pay for it. (All the statistics we build in this book and on our website use public data as inputs.) That hurts our ability to test assumptions or duplicate results. Second, over the years it has become apparent that there's quite a bit of "noise" in zone-based fielding analysis. Sometimes the conclusions drawn from zone data don't hold up to scrutiny, and sometimes the different data provided by different providers don't look anything alike, giving wildly different results. Sometimes the hard-working professional stringers or scorers might unknowingly inflict unconscious bias into the mix: for example good fielders will often be credited with more expected outs despite the data, and ballparks with high press boxes tend to score more line drives than ones with a lower press box.

Enter our Fielding Runs Above Average (FRAA). For most positions, FRAA is built from play-by-play data, which allows us to avoid the subjectivity found in many other fielding metrics. The idea is this: count how many fielding plays are made by a given player and compare that to expected plays for an average fielder at their position (based on pitcher ground ball tendencies and batter handedness). Then we adjust for park and base-out situations.

When it comes to catchers, our methodology is a little different thanks to the laundry list of responsibilities they're tasked with beyond just, well, catching and throwing the ball. By now you've probably heard about "framing" or the art of making umpires more likely to call balls outside the strike zone for strikes. To put this into one tidy number, we incorporate pitch tracking data (for the years it exists) and adjust for important factors like pitcher, umpire, batter and home-field advantage using a mixed-model approach. This grants us a number for how many strikes the catcher is personally adding to (or subtracting from) his pitchers' performance...which we then convert to runs added or lost using linear weights.

Framing is one of the biggest parts of determining catcher value, but we also take into account blocking balls from going past, whether a scorer deems it a passed ball or a wild pitch. We use a similar approach—one that really benefits from the pitch tracking data that tells us what ends up in the dirt and what doesn't. We also include a catcher's ability to prevent stolen bases and how well they field balls in play, and *finally* we come up with our FRAA for catchers.

Pitching

Both pitching and fielding make up the half of baseball that isn't run scoring: run prevention. Separating pitching from fielding is a tough task, and most recent pitching analysis has branched off from Voros McCracken's famous (and controversial) statement, "There is little if any difference among major-league pitchers in their ability to prevent hits on balls hit in the field of play." The research of the analytic community has validated this to some extent, and there are a host of "defense-independent" pitching measures that have been developed to try and extract the effect of the defense behind a hurler from the pitcher's work.

Our solution to this quandary is Deserved Run Average (DRA), our core pitching metric. DRA looks like earned run average (ERA), the tried-and-true pitching stat you've seen on every baseball broadcast or box score from the past century, but it's very different. To start, DRA takes an event-by-event look at what the pitchers does, and adjusts the value of that event based on different environmental factors like park, batter, catcher, umpire, base-out situation, run differential, inning, defense, home field advantage, pitcher role and temperature. That mixed model gives us a pitcher's expected contribution, similar to what we do for our DRC+ model for hitters and FRAA model for catchers. (Oh, and we also consider the pitcher's effect on basestealing and on balls getting past the catcher.)

It's important to note that DRA is set to the scale of runs allowed per nine innings (RA9) instead of ERA, which makes DRA's scale slightly higher than ERA's. The reason for this is because ERA tends to overrate three types of pitchers:

1. Pitchers who play in parks where scorers hand out more errors. Official scorers differ significantly in the frequency at which they assign errors to fielders.
2. Ground-ball pitchers, because a substantial proportion of errors occur on groundballs.
3. Pitchers who aren't very good. Better pitchers often allow fewer unearned runs than bad pitchers, because good pitchers tend to find ways to get out of jams.

Since the last time you picked up an edition of this book, we've also made a few minor changes to DRA to make it better. Recent research into "tunneling"—the act of throwing consecutive pitches that appear similar from a batter's point of view until after the swing decision point–data has given us a new contextual factor to account for in DRA: plate distance. This refers to the distance between successive pitches as they approach the plate, and while it has a smaller effect than factors like velocity or whiff rate, it still can help explain pitcher strikeout rate in our model.

New Pitching Metrics for 2020

We're including a few "new" pitching metrics in the book for the 2020 edition, though unlike last year, these numbers may be a little bit more familiar to those of you who have spent some time investigating baseball statistics.

Fastball Percentage

Our fastball percentage (FB%) statistic measures how frequently a pitcher throws a pitch classified as a "fastball," measured as a percentage of overall pitches thrown. We qualify three types of fastballs:

1. The traditional four-seam fastball;
2. The two-seam fastball or sinker;
3. "Hard cutters," which are pitches that have the movement profile of a cut fastball and are used as the pitcher's primary offering or in place of a more traditional fastball.

For example, a pitcher with a FB% of 67 throws any combination of these three pitches about two-thirds of the time.

Whiff Rate

Everybody loves a swing and a miss, and whiff rate (WHF) measures how frequently pitchers induce a swinging strike. To calculate WHF, we add up all the pitches thrown that ended with a swinging strike, then divide that number by a pitcher's total pitches thrown. Most often, high whiff rates correlate with high strikeout rates (and overall effective pitcher performance).

Called Strike Probability

Called Strike Probability (CSP) is a number that represents the likelihood that all of a pitcher's pitches will be called a strike while controlling for location, pitcher and batter handedness, umpire and count. Here's how it works: on each pitch, our model determines how many times (out of 100) that a similar pitch was called for a strike given those factors mentioned above, and when normalized for each batter's strike zone. Then we average the CSP for all pitches thrown by a pitcher in a season, and that gives us the yearly CSP percentage you see in the stats boxes.

As you might imagine, pitchers with a higher CSP are more likely to work in the zone, where pitchers with a lower CSP are likely locating their pitches outside the normal strike zone, for better or for worse.

Projections

Many of you aren't turning to this book just for a look at what a player has done, but for a look at what a player is going to do: the PECOTA projections. PECOTA, initially developed by Nate Silver (who has moved on to greater fame as a political analyst), consists of three parts:

1. Major-league equivalencies, which use minor-league statistics to project how a player will perform in the major leagues;
2. Baseline forecasts, which use weighted averages and regression to the mean to estimate a player's current true talent level; and
3. Aging curves, which uses the career paths of comparable players to estimate how a player's statistics are likely to change over time.

With all those important things covered, let's take a look at what's in the book this year.

Team Prospectus

Most of this book is composed of team chapters, with one for each of the 30 major-league franchises. On the first page of each chapter, you'll see a box that contains some of the key statistics for each team as well as a very inviting stadium diagram. (You can see an example of this for the Milwaukee Brewers on this very page!)

We start with the team name, their unadjusted 2019 win-loss record, and their divisional ranking. Beneath that are a host of other team statistics. **Pythag** presents an adjusted 2019 winning percentage, calculated by taking runs scored per game (**RS/G**) and runs allowed per game (**RA/G**) for the team, and running them through a version of Bill James' Pythagorean formula that was refined and improved by David Smyth and Brandon Heipp. (The formula is called "Pythagenpat," which is equally fun to type and to say.)

Next up is **DRC+**, described earlier, to indicate the overall hitting ability of the team either above or below league-average. Run prevention on the pitching side is covered by **DRA** (also mentioned earlier) and another metric: Fielding Independent Pitching (**FIP**), which calculates another ERA-like statistic based on strikeouts, walks, and home runs recorded. Defensive Efficiency Rating (**DER**) tells us the percentage of balls in play turned into outs for the team, and is a quick fielding shorthand that rounds out run prevention.

After that, we have several measures related to roster composition, as opposed to on-field performance. **B-Age** and **P-Age** tell us the average age of a team's batters and pitchers, respectively. **Salary** is the combined team payroll for all on-field players, and Doug Pappas' Marginal Dollars per Marginal Win (**M$/MW**) tells us how much money a team spent to earn production above replacement level.

Ending this batch of statistics is the number of disabled list days a team had over the season (**IL Days**) and the amount of salary paid to players on the disabled list (**$ on IL**); this final number is expressed as a percentage of total payroll.

Next to each of these stats, we've listed each team's MLB rank in that category from first to 30th. In this, first always indicates a positive outcome and 30th a negative outcome, except in the case of salary—first is highest.

After the franchise statistics, we share a few items about the team's home ballpark. There's the aforementioned diagram of the park's dimensions (including distances to the outfield wall), a graphic showing the height of the wall from the left-field pole to the right-field pole, and a table showing three-year park factors for the stadium. The park factors are displayed as indexes where 100 is average, 110 means that the park inflates the statistic in question by 10 percent, and 90 means that the park deflates the statistic in question by 10 percent.

On the second page of each team chapter, you'll find three graphs. The first is the **2019 Hit List Ranking**. This shows our Hit List Rank for the team on each day of the 2019 season and is intended to give you a picture of the ups and downs of the team's season. Hit List Rank measures overall team performance and drives the Hit List Power Rankings at the baseballprospectus.com website.

The second graph is **Committed Payroll** and helps you see how the team's payroll has compared to the MLB and divisional average payrolls over time. Payroll figures are current as of January 1, 2020; with so many free agents still unsigned as of this writing, the final 2020 figure will likely be significantly different for many teams. (In the meantime, you can always find the most current data at Baseball Prospectus' Cot's Baseball Contracts page.)

The third graph is **Farm System Ranking** and displays how the Baseball Prospectus prospect team has ranked the organization's farm system since 2007.

After the graphs, we have a **Personnel** section that lists many of the important decision-makers and upper-level field and operations staff members for the franchise, as well as any former Baseball Prospectus staff members who are currently part of the organization. (In very rare circumstances, someone might be on both lists!)

Juan Soto LF

Born: 10/25/98   Age: 21   Bats: L   Throws: L
Height: 6'1"   Weight: 185   Origin: International Free Agent, 2015

YEAR	TEAM	LVL	AGE	PA	R	2B	3B	HR	RBI	BB	K	SB	CS	AVG/OBP/SLG
2017	NAT	RK	18	27	3	1	1	0	4	2	1	0	0	.320/.370/.440
2017	HAG	A	18	96	15	5	0	3	14	10	8	1	2	.360/.427/.523
2018	HAG	A	19	74	12	5	3	5	24	14	13	2	0	.373/.486/.814
2018	POT	A+	19	73	17	3	1	7	18	11	8	0	1	.371/.466/.790
2018	HAR	AA	19	35	4	2	0	2	10	4	7	1	0	.323/.400/.581
2018	WAS	MLB	19	494	77	25	1	22	70	79	99	5	2	.292/.406/.517
2019	WAS	MLB	20	659	110	32	5	34	110	108	132	12	1	.282/.401/.548
2020	WAS	MLB	21	630	92	30	3	35	102	85	123	5	2	.284/.382/.543

Comparables: Ronald Acuña Jr., Mike Trout, Tony Conigliaro

YEAR	TEAM	LVL	AGE	PA	DRC+	VORP	BABIP	BRR	FRAA	WARP
2017	NAT	RK	18	27	135	1.5	.333	0.0	RF(9): -1.1	0.0
2017	HAG	A	18	96	181	8.0	.373	1.0	RF(19): -1.9, LF(2): -0.3	0.9
2018	HAG	A	19	74	222	14.5	.405	0.3	RF(14): 1.1, CF(2): 0.2	1.2
2018	POT	A+	19	73	260	15.4	.340	1.4	RF(14): 1.0, LF(1): 0.0	1.6
2018	HAR	AA	19	35	113	3.6	.364	0.0	LF(4): 0.6, RF(4): -0.5	0.1
2018	WAS	MLB	19	494	125	40.5	.338	-0.5	LF(114): 2.7	3.0
2019	WAS	MLB	20	659	136	49.0	.312	1.4	LF(150): -0.8	4.9
2020	WAS	MLB	21	630	133	43.6	.310	-0.1	LF 3	4.8

Position Players

After all that information and a thoughtful bylined essay covering each team, we present our player comments. These are also bylined, but due to frequent franchise shifts during the offseason, our bylines are more a rough guide than a perfect accounting of who wrote what.

Each player is listed with the major-league team that employed him as of early January 2020. If a player changed teams after that point via free agency, trade, or any other method, you'll be able to find them in the chapter for their previous squad.

As an example, take a look at the player comment for Nationals outfielder Juan Soto: the stat block that accompanies his written comment is at the top of this page. First we cover biographical information (age is as of June 30, 2020) before moving onto the stats themselves. Our statistic columns include standard identifying information like **YEAR**, **TEAM**, **LVL** (level of affiliated play) and **AGE** before getting into the numbers. Next, we provide raw, untranslated numbers like you might find on the back of your dad's baseball cards: **PA** (plate appearances), **R** (runs), **2B** (doubles), **3B** (triples), **HR** (home runs), **RBI** (runs batted in), **BB** (walks), **K** (strikeouts), **SB** (stolen bases) and **CS** (caught stealing).

Next, we have unadjusted "slash" statistics: **AVG** (batting average), **OBP** (on-base percentage) and **SLG** (slugging percentage). Following the slash line is **DRC+** (Deserved Runs Created Plus), which we described earlier as total offensive expected contribution compared to the league average.

One of our oldest active metrics, **VORP** (Value Over Replacement Player), considers offensive production, position and plate appearances. In essence, it is the number of runs contributed beyond what a replacement-level player at the same position would contribute if given the same percentage of team plate appearances. VORP does not consider the quality of a player's defense.

BABIP (batting average on balls in play) tells us how often a ball in play fell for a hit, and can help us identify whether a batter may have been lucky or not…but note that high BABIPs also tend to follow the great hitters of our time, as well as speedy singles hitters who put the ball on the ground.

The next item is **BRR** (Baserunning Runs), which covers all of a player's baserunning accomplishments including (but not limited to) swiped bags and failed attempts. Next is **FRAA** (Fielding Runs Above Average), which also includes the number of games previously played at each position noted in parentheses. Multi-position players have only their two most frequent positions listed here, but their total FRAA number reflects all positions played.

Our last column here is **WARP** (Wins Above Replacement Player). WARP estimates the total value of a player, which means for hitters it takes into account hitting runs above average (calculated using the DRC+ model), BRR and FRAA. Then, it makes an adjustment for positions played and gives the player a credit for plate appearances based upon the difference between "replacement level"—which is derived from the quality of players added to a team's roster after the start of the season–and the league average.

The final line just below the stats box is **PECOTA** data, which is discussed further in a following section.

Catchers

Catchers are a special breed, and thus they have earned their own separate box which displays some of the defensive metrics that we've built just for them. As an example, let's check out J.T. Realmuto.

The **YEAR** and **TEAM** columns match what you'd find in the other stat box. **P. COUNT** indicates the number of pitches thrown while the catcher was behind the plate, including swinging strikes, fouls and balls in play. **FRM RUNS** is the total run value the catcher provided (or cost) his team by influencing the umpire to call strikes where other catchers did not. **BLK RUNS** expresses the total run value above or below average for the catcher's ability to prevent wild pitches and passed balls. **THRW RUNS** is calculated using a similar model as the previous two statistics, and it measures a catcher's ability to throw out basestealers but also to dissuade them from testing his arm in the first place. It takes into account factors like the pitcher (including his delivery and pickoff move) and baserunner (who could be as fast as Billy Hamilton or as slow as Yonder Alonso). **TOT RUNS** is the sum of all of the previous three statistics.

Justin Verlander   RHP
Born: 02/20/83   Age: 37   Bats: R   Throws: R
Height: 6'5"   Weight: 225   Origin: Round 1, 2004 Draft (#2 overall)

YEAR	TEAM	LVL	AGE	W	L	SV	G	GS	IP	H	HR	BB/9	K/9	K	GB%	BABIP
2017	DET	MLB	34	10	8	0	28	28	172	153	23	3.5	9.2	176	34%	.283
2017	HOU	MLB	34	5	0	0	5	5	34	17	4	1.3	11.4	43	32%	.194
2018	HOU	MLB	35	16	9	0	34	34	214	156	28	1.6	12.2	290	31%	.272
2019	HOU	MLB	36	21	6	0	34	34	223	137	36	1.7	12.1	300	36%	.219
2020	HOU	MLB	37	15	6	0	29	29	184	138	28	2.3	12.1	248	35%	.274

Comparables: Zack Greinke, A.J. Burnett, Aníbal Sánchez

YEAR	TEAM	LVL	AGE	WHIP	ERA	DRA	WARP	MPH	FB%	WHF	CSP
2017	DET	MLB	34	1.28	3.82	4.03	3.0	97.7	58	11	47.8
2017	HOU	MLB	34	0.65	1.06	3.08	0.9	97.5	59.6	15.1	49.9
2018	HOU	MLB	35	0.90	2.52	2.33	7.3	97.5	61.2	16.2	51.6
2019	HOU	MLB	36	0.80	2.58	2.51	7.9	96.8	49.9	17.5	48.3
2020	HOU	MLB	37	1.01	2.75	2.95	5.3	95.8	54.6	15.1	48.2

Pitchers

Let's give our pitchers a turn, using 2019 AL Cy Young winner Justin Verlander as our example. Take a look at his stat block: the first line and the **YEAR**, **TEAM**, **LVL** and **AGE** columns are the same as in the position player example earlier.

Here too, we have a series of columns that display raw, unadjusted statistics compiled by the pitcher over the course of a season: **W** (wins), **L** (losses), **SV** (saves), **G** (games pitched), **GS** (games started), **IP** (innings pitched), **H** (hits allowed) and **HR** (home runs allowed). Next we have two statistics that are rates: **BB/9** (walks per nine innings) and **K/9** (strikeouts per nine innings), before returning to the unadjusted K (strikeouts).

Next up is **GB%** (ground ball percentage), which is the percentage of all batted balls that were hit on the ground, including both outs and hits. Remember, this is based on observational data and subject to human error, so please approach this with a healthy dose of skepticism.

BABIP (batting average on balls in play) is calculated using the same methodology as it is for position players, but it often tells us more about a pitcher than it does a hitter. With pitchers, a high BABIP is often due to poor defense or bad luck, and can often be an indicator of potential rebound, and a low BABIP may be cause to expect performance regression. (A typical league-average BABIP is close to .290-.300.)

Baltimore Orioles 2020

The metrics **WHIP** (walks plus hits per inning pitched) and **ERA** (earned run average) are old standbys: WHIP measures walks and hits allowed on a per-inning basis, while ERA measures earned runs on a nine-inning basis. Neither of these stats are translated or adjusted.

DRA (Deserved Run Average) was described at length earlier, and measures how many runs the pitcher "deserved" to allow per nine innings. Please note that since we lack all the data points that would make for a "real" DRA for minor-league events, the DRA displayed for minor league partial-seasons is based off of different data. (That data is a modified version of our cFIP metric, which you can find more information about on our website.)

Just like with hitters, **WARP** (Wins Above Replacement Player) is a total value metric that puts pitchers of all stripes on the same scale as position players. We use DRA as the primary input for our calculation of WARP. You might notice that relief pitchers (due to their limited innings) may have a lower WARP than you were expecting or than you might see in other WARP-like metrics. WARP does not take leverage into account, just the actions a pitcher performs and the expected value of those actions...which ends up judging high-leverage relief pitchers differently than you might imagine given their prestige and market value.

MPH gives you the pitcher's 95th percentile velocity for the noted season, in order to give you an idea of what the *peak* fastball velocity a pitcher possesses. Since this comes from our pitch-tracking data, it is not publicly available for minor-league pitchers.

Finally, we display the three new pitching metrics we described earlier. **FB%** (fastball percentage) gives you the percentage of fastballs thrown out of all pitches. **WHF** (whiff rate) tells you the percentage of swinging strikes induced out of all pitches. **CSP** (called strike probability) expresses the likelihood of all pitches thrown to result in a called strike, after controlling for factors like handedness, umpire, pitch type, count and location.

PECOTA

All players have PECOTA projections for 2020, as well as a set of other numbers that describe the performance of comparable players according to PECOTA. All projections for 2020 are for the player at the date we went to press in early January and are projected into the league and park context as indicated by the team abbreviation. (Note that players at very low levels of the minors are too unpredictable to assess using these numbers.) All PECOTA projected statistics represent a player's projected major-league performance.

Below the projections are the player's three highest-scoring comparable players as determined by PECOTA. All comparables represent a snapshot of how the listed player was performing at the same age as the current player, so if a

23-year-old pitcher is compared to Bartolo Colón, he's actually being compared to a 23-year-old Colón, not the version that pitched for the Rangers in 2018, nor to Colón's career as a whole.

A few points about pitcher projections. First, we aren't yet projecting peak velocity, so that column will be blank in the PECOTA lines. Second, projecting DRA is trickier than evaluating past performance, because it is unclear how deserving each pitcher will be of his anticipated outcomes. However, we know that another DRA-related statistic–contextual FIP or cFIP–estimates future run scoring very well. So for PECOTA, the projected DRA figures you see are based on the past cFIPs generated by the pitcher and comparable players over time, along with the other factors described above.

Lineouts

In each chapter's Lineouts section, you'll find abbreviated text comments, as well as all the same information you'd find in our full player comments. The only difference is that we limit the stats boxes in this section to only including the 2019 information for each player.

Managers

After all those wonderful team chapters, we've got statistics for each big-league manager, all of whom are organized by alphabetical order. Here you'll find a block including an extraordinary amount of information collected from each manager's entire career. For more information on the acronyms and what they mean, please visit the Glossary at www.baseballprospectus.com.

There is one important metric that we'd like to call attention to, and you'll find it next to each manager's name: **wRM+** (weighted reliever management plus). Developed by Rob Arthur and Rian Watt, wRM+ investigates how good a manager is at using their best relievers during the moments of highest leverage, using both our proprietary DRA metric as well as Leverage Index. wRM+ is scaled to a league average of 100, and a wRM+ of 105 indicates that relievers were used approximately five percent "better" than average. On the other hand, a wRM+ of 95 would tell us the team used its relievers five percent "worse" than the average team.

While wRM+ does not have an extremely strong correlation with a manager, it is statistically significant; this means that a manager is not *entirely* responsible for a team's wRM+, but does have some effect on that number.

PECOTA Leaderboards

If you're familiar with PECOTA, then you'll have noticed that the projection system often appears bullish on players coming off a bad year and bearish on players coming off a good year. (This is because the system weights several previous seasons, not just the most recent one.) In addition, we publish the 50th

Baltimore Orioles 2020

percentile projections for each player–which is smack in the middle of the range of projected production—which tends to mean PECOTA stat lines don't often have extreme results like 40 home runs or 250 strikeouts in a given season. In essence, PECOTA doesn't project very many extreme seasons.

At the end of the book, we've ranked the top players at each position based on their PECOTA projections. This might help you visualize just how a given player's projection compares to that of their peers, so that even if a dramatic stat line isn't projected, you can still imagine how they stack up against the rest of the league.

Part 1: Team Analysis

Baltimore Orioles: Where Are You Going, Where Have You Been?

Derek Albin, Jeffrey Paternostro and Matthew Trueblood

2019: What Went Right
Was anything supposed to go right for Baltimore in the first place? PECOTA projected them to win 59 games, after all. They fell short of that forecast, and yet, it wasn't all bad last season. For a team in the early stages of a rebuild, it's important to self-evaluate. There are players on the team's current 40-man roster who will be a part of the next winning Orioles club. There were also players who showed enough to be used in trades to advance the rebuild. From that standpoint, the Orioles were mildly successful with a few different bats. Although the team's 88 DRC+ was fourth-worst in the majors, Trey Mancini, Jonathan Villar, Renato Núñez, Hanser Alberto, and Anthony Santander were strong contributors, at least within the context of the overall team.

Mancini led the team with 35 homers and 120 DRC+. The 27-year-old rebounded from a rough 2018 and became the subject of trade rumors. Though the Orioles held onto him, it wouldn't be surprising to see him move before the end of the current season. Mancini is first-time arbitration eligible this winter, so the combination of encroaching age and increasing salary minimizes the chances of him being on the next good Baltimore team. Villar is already gone; his 94 DRC+ wasn't spectacular, but he does provide good pop for a middle infielder and is a base-stealing threat. He'd had an indifferent career up until 2019, save for a 2.7 WARP 2016 season in Milwaukee (which he exceeded in 2019). Having watched him rebuild his value on the verge of free agency, the Orioles sent him off to Miami.

It wasn't just players destined for the trade block who did well for Baltimore; a handful of useful bats emerged as well. Núñez, who's bounced around in his young career, took advantage of his opportunity. Despite a meager 83 DRC+ PECOTA projection, the 25-year-old DH has posted a 99 mark along with 31 dingers. He needs to reach base a little more often, but there might be a long-term role here for him. Alberto, who Baltimore claimed off waivers twice prior to the season, was a steady presence in the infield. His .305 batting average, infield versatility, and 98 DRC+ earned the 27-year-old a part in this club's future. Santander, who had a one-game cameo in early May before rejoining the team for good in June, posted the fourth-highest WARP on the team despite playing in just 93 games.

The Orioles didn't have quite as much good fortune on the mound, but one pitcher emerged. Lefty John Means was Baltimore's lone All-Star, primarily because they had to have at least one. Even though he's not a frontline starter, he rode his changeup to some success this year (3.60 ERA, 4.61 DRA). That DRA may not look pretty, but it is about five percent better than average. All told, Means shattered PECOTA's expectations (5.55 ERA, 5.45 DRA) and could be a staple in the back of Baltimore's rotation. That is if they had any frontline starters. He'll have to remain the club's de facto ace.

Andrew Cashner delivered 96 strong innings before Baltimore traded him to the Red Sox. It seemed like the righty was a lost cause after a 6.69 DRA and -2.4 WARP in 2018, but instead, he delivered a 3.83 ERA. The Orioles received two rookie-level prospects for Cashner, which doesn't sound like much, but it's certainly better than what anyone could have anticipated prior to 2019.

2019: What Went Wrong

It's difficult to disappoint when expectations are already so low. Sure, the Orioles exceeded their 2018 record (47-115), but there were still a few developmental goals that didn't come to fruition along with some awful individual performances. To get the obvious out of the way, Chris Davis was dreadful. The first baseman didn't get his first hit until April 14th, which ended a stretch of futility that dated back to the previous September. Things didn't get much better from there, with Davis—a bat-first first baseman—finishing at .179/.276/.326, equivalent to a paltry 65 DRC+.

More problematic than Davis were a few young players who failed to establish themselves. Cedric Mullins was supposed to take over center field for the departed Adam Jones. Unfortunately, after a brutal 74 plate appearances (55 DRC+), he was demoted to the minors for good. To make matters worse, he continued to scuffle in Triple-A and was sent down to Double-A in July.

If you a) throw a ball off the mound, b) play for the Orioles, and c) aren't John Means…well, you're part of the problem. The Orioles set the single-season record for home runs allowed (305), but in spite of that, the staff's DRA ranked just seventh-worst in all of baseball. Trading Cashner mid-season certainly didn't help and the absence of Alex Cobb, who made just three starts all season, hurt too. Perhaps most frustrating, though, was Dylan Bundy's season. PECOTA expected a modest but respectable year from the righty and called for a 4.59 ERA and 4.46 DRA entering 2019. So much for that, and so much for Bundy and the team's protracted battle to salvage value from the fourth-overall pick of the 2011 draft; he now belongs to the Angels.

Last but not least, this section wouldn't be complete without mentioning Gleyber Torres. Plenty of hitters feasted against Baltimore, but none more than Torres, who hit 13 homers and recorded a 1.512 OPS in 75 trips to the plate. The unresolvable question: Was Torres *that* good, or was Orioles pitching *that* bad? A: Maybe both. —*Derek Albin*

Prospect Outlook

The Orioles used 39 pitchers in 2019. The lowest HR/9 among rotation regulars was 1.0. Their All-Star, Means, posted a 1.3. They need pitching help. **Ryan Mountcastle** is closer to the majors than their bevy of upper minors arms, and a better prospect, but adding another good corner bat to Trey Mancini isn't going to move the needle here. Whether it's **Michael Baumann**, **Alex Wells**, **Dean Kremer**, **Zac Lowther**, **Bruce Zimmerman**, or **Keegan Akin**...well, you might end up seeing all of them. Wells has some Means in the profile, but as Daffy Duck said, "It's a nice trick, but I can only do it once." Zimmerman isn't quite as good as Wells, but broadly similar. Baumann has a starter's frame, but maybe not a starter's out pitch. We've seen how that goes in Camden. Kremer, Akin, and Lowther might be better suited to relief. You'd think one or two of these arms turn into viable major league starters, but it also isn't exactly a crop of prospects as good as Chris Tillman, Kevin Gausman, Brian Matusz, and Dylan Bundy.

There is help further down. Both RHP **Grayson Rodriguez** and LHP **DL Hall** rank among the team's 10 best prospects. No. 1 overall pick **Adley Rutschman** is a big name at the top of the system, but it's thin one for bats overall: **Yusniel Díaz** has scuffled a bit, and **Ryan McKenna** has some fourth outfielder markers on his profile. Overall, the system is improving, and the Orioles have a lot of arms to throw at their gopher-ball issues, but it's not clear it's going to be much better any time soon. You'd hope the system would be a bit better than average-ish at this point in the rebuild. —*Jeffrey Paternostro*

2020 Outlook

There's a fair chance that RHP Brandon Bailey, who GM Mike Elias's new team selected from his old one in the Rule 5 Draft in December, will open the season in Baltimore's starting rotation. That says most of what needs saying, not only about the Orioles' overall predicament, but about their efforts to ameliorate it any time soon. Swapping Villar and Bundy for prospects without name value or proximity to the majors made clear what Elias and company intend for the 2020 O's, and that makes sense. It's also a strategy that both the arbitrage-era Astros and the quick-rebuild Brewers (under fellow former Houston man David Stearns) employed to great effect, so it might pay off in unexpected ways.

Baltimore Orioles 2020

In the meantime, very little lipstick has been applied to the pig. José Iglesias was a nice pickup, an excellent fielder at shortstop who replaces Villar and should be good for the development of any pitchers Baltimore can fish out of the corners of its still-middling farm. One can't help but observe, however, that Villar is a very versatile player, and that adding Iglesias could have been done without dumping Villar's salary for a low-wattage trade return. —*Matthew Trueblood*

Performance Graphs

2019 Hit List Ranking

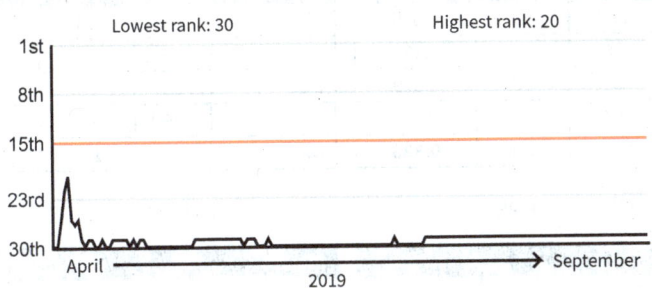

Committed Payroll (in millions)

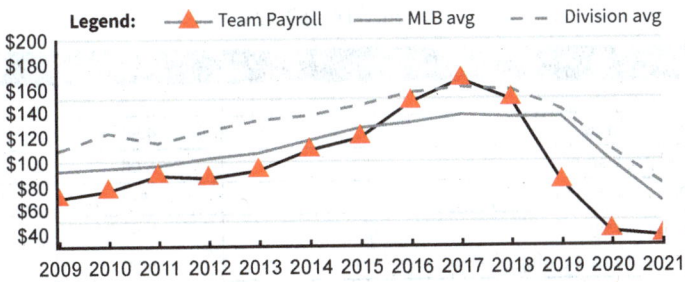

Farm System Ranking

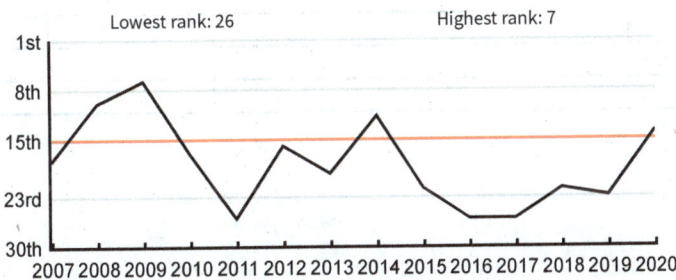

2019 Team Performance

ACTUAL STANDINGS

Team	W	L	Pct
NYA	103	59	0.636
TBA	96	66	0.593
BOS	84	78	0.519
TOR	67	95	0.414
BAL	54	108	0.333

THIRD-ORDER STANDINGS

Team	W	L	Pct
TBA	99	63	0.613
NYA	96	66	0.590
BOS	88	74	0.544
TOR	66	96	0.410
BAL	59	103	0.363

TOP HITTERS

Player	WARP
Jonathan Villar	3.3
Trey Mancini	2.8
Hanser Alberto	2.0

TOP PITCHERS

Player	WARP
John Means	1.9
Dylan Bundy	1.6
Mychal Givens	1.6

VITAL STATISTICS

Statistic Name	Value	Rank
Pythagenpat	.358	29th
Runs Scored per Game	4.50	22nd
Runs Allowed per Game	6.06	30th
Deserved Runs Created Plus	88	26th
Deserved Run Average	5.52	24th
Fielding Independent Pitching	5.59	30th
Defensive Efficiency Rating	.705	13th
Batter Age	26.5	3rd
Pitcher Age	27.2	7th
Salary	$80.8M	27th
Marginal $ per Marginal Win	$12.5M	2nd
Injured List Days	924	7th
$ on IL	32%	28th

2020 Team Projections

PROJECTED STANDINGS

Team	W	L	Pct	+/-
NYA	99.0	63.0	0.611	-4
TBA	87.3	74.7	0.539	-9
BOS	84.5	77.5	0.522	0
TOR	76.6	85.4	0.473	10
BAL	**62.9**	**99.1**	**0.388**	**9**

TOP PROJECTED HITTERS

Player	WARP
Trey Mancini	2.0
Austin Hays	1.4
Anthony Santander	1.3

TOP PROJECTED PITCHERS

Player	WARP
John Means	2.2
Mychal Givens	0.7
Dean Kremer	0.6

FARM SYSTEM REPORT

Top Prospect	Number of Top 101 Prospects
Adley Rutschman, #4	3

KEY DEDUCTIONS

Player	WARP
Jonathan Villar	1.1
Dylan Bundy	0.5

KEY ADDITIONS

Player	WARP
José Iglesias	1.2
Dean Kremer	0.6
Michael Baumann	0.6
Zac Lowther	0.5
Brandon Bailey	0.3
Keegan Akin	0.1
Yusniel Díaz	0.0
Ryan Mountcastle	0.0
Ryan McKenna	0.0
Pat Valaika	0.0

Team Personnel

Executive Vice President and General Manager
Mike Elias

Vice President & Assistant General Manager, Analytics
Sig Mejdal

Director, Baseball Administration
Kevin Buck

Director, Player Development
Matt Blood

Manager
Brandon Hyde

BP Alumni
Kevin Carter

Oriole Park at Camden Yards Stats

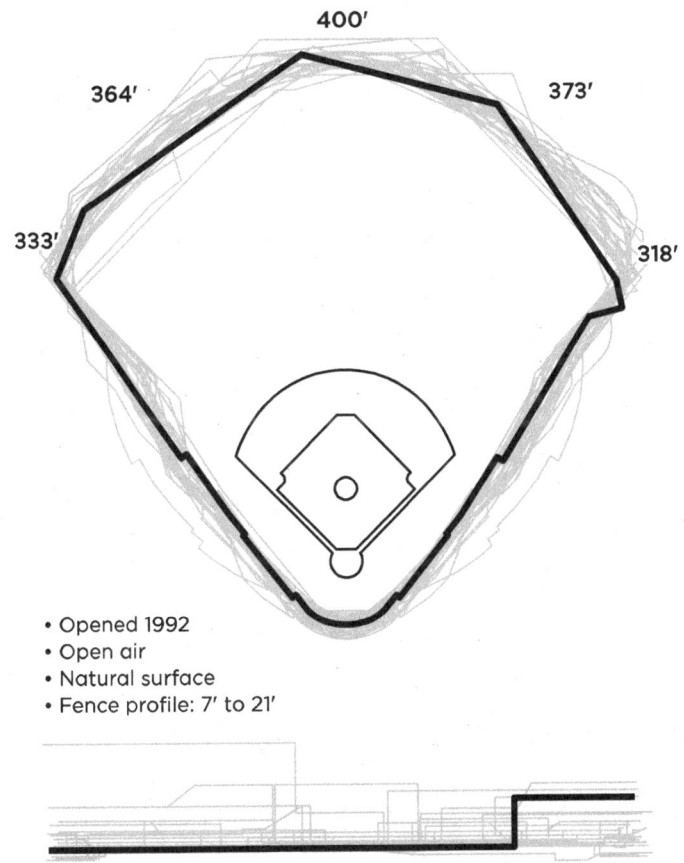

- Opened 1992
- Open air
- Natural surface
- Fence profile: 7' to 21'

Three-Year Park Factors

Runs	Runs/RH	Runs/LH	HR/RH	HR/LH
101	102	100	111	106

Orioles Team Analysis

I remember standing in the upper deck at Camden Yards on May 11, 2015. The stadium was packed and the crowd swelled with anticipation ahead of the first home game since the protests against police brutality that brought Baltimore to its knees. I still get emotional about that day, and how it transported me back to my post-9/11 New Jersey childhood, when I first learned what a baseball team can mean to a place—how it can stitch together a city torn apart at the seams.

Along with many other residents instructed to remain indoors, I watched the April 29th game on television. You might recall that game as the empty-stadium contest played by the Orioles and Chicago White Sox. Even then, as each bat crack and slapped mitt echoed around the ballpark, I thought I was experiencing something I would never see again.

Over the intervening years, I went to countless Orioles games. The team and the open arms of Camden Yards kept me company during my time in graduate school. During one otherwise forgettable weekday game in June of 2019—one of the last games I would attend before leaving Baltimore—a thought passed through my mind: "This place is a ghost town." The stadium was almost as quiet as it had been on that April afternoon.

Just as the city had attempted to rebuild years prior, now its baseball team has to as well.

⚾ ⚾ ⚾

Of the players on those 2015 Orioles, only Chris Davis and Mychal Givens remain. Gone are the days of Adam Jones and Manny Machado, as the franchise has sped away from the Buck Showalter era. This is instead Mike Elias and Brandon Hyde's time to...well, not shine, not yet.

I don't want to dwell too much on the negative aspects of the 2019 Orioles—and there were many, to be clear, including yielding a record amount of home runs. Every season, even a 108-loss effort, contains within it nuggets of joy. To wit: John Means' star rose bright across the night sky that was the majors' worst pitching staff; Jonathan Villar, Trey Mancini and Hanser Alberto all gave fans reasons to keep watching when the Orioles were at the dish; Stevie Wilkerson recorded the first save by a position player in the history of the game,

Baltimore Orioles 2020

and then recorded arguably the best catch of the year during the season finale. (It was an exciting game, for those who didn't watch it. The Orioles lost, which you probably guessed. So it goes.)

It's eternally tempting to lean into those negative aspects because of the circumstances at play. After all, as the Orioles suffered through their second consecutive 100-loss season in 2019, their Beltway rivals celebrated their first World Series victory—and did so while embracing a player who had come up short during his time in Baltimore. But hey, Gerardo Parra, cult hero, was simply a dash of salt in the protracted wound for most Orioles fans.

The reality is that this is not the upstart team down the road in the nation's capital—still a fledgling in baseball years. This is not the headline-grabbing, All-American championship squad. This is standing resolute, with a chip on your shoulder and knowing the difficult road ahead. This is Birdland. And right now, Birdland is a tough place to be—partially by design.

The Orioles continued to dismantle their old core over the winter, trading Dylan Bundy and non-tendering Jonathan Villar. Heading into 2020, there's a tacit agreement in place: play well, and you'll probably find yourself traded—especially if you make more than the league-minimum salary. That could mean the likes of Mancini and—yes—Givens go next.

Were it not for Chris Davis' immovable deal, the Orioles payroll would likely sit well below its current $60 million projection.

⚾ ⚾ ⚾

"I want to see a playoff team at Camden Yards, and we want to see a playoff team at Camden Yards," Elias said in the aftermath of the Villar and Bundy moves. "There's only one way to get there, given where we're at, where we're starting from. We all know the strategy, the process. This is not easy. This is not something we want to happen again, but coming into the organization in late 2018, with the roster construction what it was, where the talent base was, where we were in the standings—this was the only path."

The only path.

When Elias says that a full teardown is "the only path," he's not offering a valid premise. Of course it wasn't the only path; tanking never is, not in an industry that prints money—not for a team that made three postseason appearances over a five-year span over the last decade. It is, however, the path that Elias—who comes direct from Houston—opted for, and it is now the path that the fan base, along with the rest of the organization, has to endure. There's no going back.

During the last homestand of the 2019 season, Orioles players wrote thank you notes to some randomly selected season ticket holders. The catharsis in the exercise was obvious. Much is made—rightly so—of the toll tanking takes on a fanbase. But it's not easy for the players either. They didn't have a choice in the matter—and still don't. They still have to show up to the ballpark every day and play, knowing that they're part of a grand exercise where their chance of signing another lease in Baltimore hinges on how well they perform—too well, and they'll find themselves on the first plane out of BWI. It could be worse; they could become known for not being good enough for a team punting the foreseeable future.

The cruel reality of a full-fledged rebuild is that it is not only the players who are perpetually on the block. The Orioles are in the midst of an organizational shakeup from top to bottom, punctuated by the firing of nearly a dozen people in the scouting department in late August, including some of whom had been with the team for decades. In a time when it feels like Moneyball has been stretched to its furthest conclusion across the sport, this is far from the most prominent or even the most cynical example of bald cost-cutting measures. But, when lifelong members of the team's community depart, a thread of Baltimore's fabric is given a gentle tug.

Ask anyone in the new Orioles regime and they will tell you there is still a lot of work to be done. Adley Rutschman, who instantly became the best prospect in the organization when the Orioles selected him with the first pick in the 2019 draft, is the first glimpse of what the future can hold. He is a switch-hitting, defensively gifted catcher who may just be everything Matt Wieters never quite was. But one top prospect, even if he develops into a superstar, does not a successful rebuild make. True, there are other reasons for optimism: Grayson Rodriguez is a promising prep pitcher with mid-rotation potential and Ryan Mountcastle posted a 115 DRC+ in Triple-A in 2019. Beyond (and arguably even including) them, many questions remain.

Look no further than last season for evidence of how quickly youngsters can see their stock collapse. Cedric Mullins ended his 2018 as Jones's heir apparent, but struggled mightily last season to remain in the plans. Yusniel Díaz, the centerpiece of the Manny Machado trade, also took a step back in 2019, as he was stymied by injury. There's a faint light at the end of the Harbor Tunnel, but it's still at the stage where you have to really squint to see it.

⚾ ⚾ ⚾

A baseball team can mean a lot to a place and to a person—in good times, and in bad, but maybe especially in bad. At its best, doing a doctorate is challenging and rewarding. It can also be incredibly isolating. When science was often fickle, baseball was always there. Camden Yards, with its gorgeous sightlines and wonderful aesthetics, was always there. Losing myself in the cadence of a game was precisely what meant the most to me when I was stretched to my mental and emotional limits.

Baltimore Orioles 2020

When we discuss "meaningful" games, we almost always mean games that have implications for the postseason. But that premise operates under the basic assumption that meaning is derived solely from winning. Rejecting that premise is smiling when you see the Orioles run out onto the field donning their weird and beautiful Maryland flag alternate jerseys. Rejecting that premise is yelling the "O!" extra loudly during the Star Spangled Banner, befuddling all of the visiting fans in the building. Rejecting that premise is sprinkling a little extra Old Bay on those crab fries. Rejecting that premise is seeking refuge at the ballpark as your city tries to heal itself, remembering that there is so much more to loving a team and loving a game than winning.

What much of the public consumes about Baltimore—the city and its baseball team—is what rises to the national headlines, much of which has been ugly. Yet the small moments embedded in the seams, from pitches thrown during a lost season, can be woven into a tapestry that tells you the story of a city lying underneath those headlines.

It can tell you the story of a city that even prior to those headlines has been decimated by systemic racism, crumbling housing and infrastructure, wage stagnation and violence. These things are unbearably isolating for those affected by them and often the only antidote is something, anything, that fosters a sense of community and supplies a rallying cry. Baltimore's communities have always been its strength. It is, after all, a city of neighborhoods, each with its own flavor and character. The cold, calculated commodification of the game and players that could have provided that sense of community and rallying cry turns baseball into a reminder of that trauma, rather than the escape it was for me all those summer nights at Camden Yards.

But I suppose baseball has always been a game that favors the journey over the destination. It meanders. It calls on you to crack open a Natty Boh and stay awhile. Baltimore is like that too. It's a rough-around-the-edges sort of place, always living in the shadow of its presently-celebrating close neighbor to the south. The longer you stay in Charm City, sitting on its stoops and walking its neighborhoods, the more apparent the aptness of the moniker becomes. Sure, investing emotionally takes work, but it is a labor of love, an exercise in passionate dedication that breeds the resilience required of an Orioles fan.

It's a bitter pill to swallow, knowing that Baltimore is a stepping stone on the way to something better. If he pitches well enough, he'll get traded to a contender. If he gets a decent enough job and starts a family, he'll leave Baltimore to live in the surrounding suburbs. What's left behind is an empty ballpark, the question hanging in the silent rows of seats: What if they stayed instead? I finished my graduate degree and I moved away from the city I had come to call home, just as the Orioles began their own journey towards something better. But just as Elias hopes to bring playoff baseball back to Baltimore, I hope I will return someday, too.

On October 15, 2014, I was finishing up an evening of experiments in the lab, listening on the radio as the Orioles were eliminated in the ALCS, bringing my first full baseball season in Baltimore to an end. It had been storming all day, but when I looked out the window next to my desk I saw a bright, beautiful rainbow arcing across the sky—a reminder that after a storm, there is hope, even if it can be fragile and fleeting.

It's a rebuild. We understand that. This was, we're told, the only path.

—*Allison McCague is an author of Baseball Prospectus.*

Part 2: Player Analysis

Baltimore Orioles 2020

PLAYER COMMENTS WITH GRAPHS

Hanser Alberto   INF
Born: 10/17/92   Age: 27   Bats: R   Throws: R
Height: 5'11"   Weight: 215   Origin: International Free Agent, 2009

YEAR	TEAM	LVL	AGE	PA	R	2B	3B	HR	RBI	BB	K	SB	CS	AVG/OBP/SLG
2018	ROU	AAA	25	384	45	17	3	7	58	9	28	0	3	.330/.346/.452
2018	TEX	MLB	25	30	0	2	0	0	0	2	4	0	1	.185/.241/.259
2019	BAL	MLB	26	550	62	21	2	12	51	16	50	4	4	.305/.329/.422
2020	BAL	MLB	27	595	58	25	2	14	65	18	68	5	3	.275/.303/.400

Comparables: Luis Sardiñas, Donovan Solano, Gio Urshela

While Alberto is an absolute delight and more-than-capable defender at three infield positions, the reason he was most useful to the Orioles will be the reason he'll be in the league for another decade if he wants to: he rakes against left-handed pitching. The only batter this century with over 200 plate appearances against southpaws to have a higher batting average against lefties than Alberto's .398 was Ichiro Suzuki in 2004. Alberto's 88 hits off lefties were the most of any player in a season, ever. After being waived by four organizations (including by the Orioles) between the end of 2018 and Opening Day 2019, a season like this will forever make Alberto a player who has a singular, exploitable skill coveted by every team, especially around playoff time. In an era of walks over hits and power over contact, Alberto's brand of late-blooming infielder is a fun throwback.

YEAR	TEAM	LVL	AGE	PA	DRC+	VORP	BABIP	BRR	FRAA	WARP
2018	ROU	AAA	25	384	111	18.4	.337	-0.8	SS(44): 7.1, 1B(43): -3.5	2.1
2018	TEX	MLB	25	30	88	-1.3	.217	-0.4	SS(5): 0.1, 2B(4): -0.1	0.0
2019	BAL	MLB	26	550	98	18.2	.318	1.6	2B(90): -5.0, 3B(66): 5.3	2.0
2020	BAL	MLB	27	595	84	11.6	.292	1.4	2B -4, 3B 1	0.9

Hanser Alberto, continued

Batted Ball Distribution

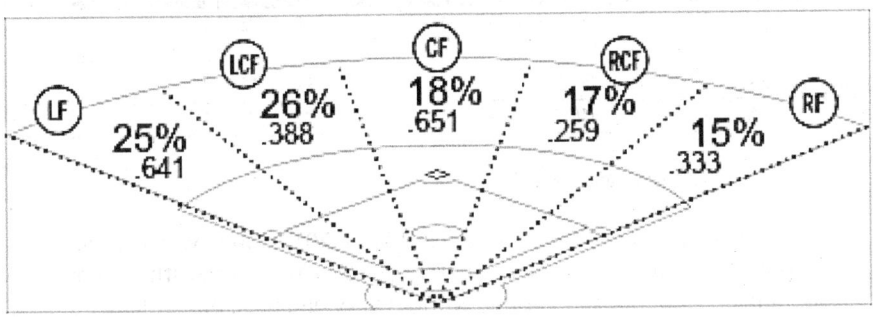

Strike Zone vs LHP   Strike Zone vs RHP

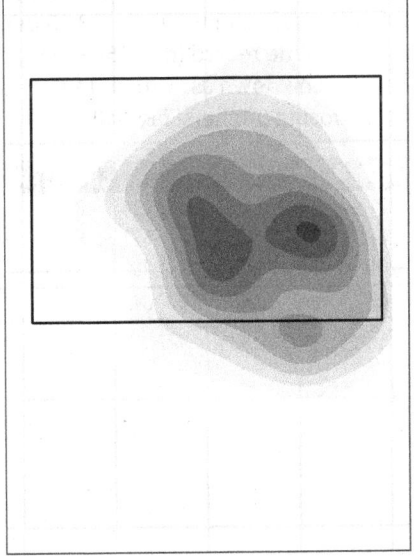

Chris Davis   1B

Born: 03/17/86   Age: 34   Bats: L   Throws: R
Height: 6'3"   Weight: 230   Origin: Round 5, 2006 Draft (#148 overall)

YEAR	TEAM	LVL	AGE	PA	R	2B	3B	HR	RBI	BB	K	SB	CS	AVG/OBP/SLG
2017	BAL	MLB	31	524	65	15	1	26	61	61	195	1	1	.215/.309/.423
2018	BAL	MLB	32	522	40	12	0	16	49	41	192	2	0	.168/.243/.296
2019	BAL	MLB	33	352	26	9	0	12	36	39	139	0	0	.179/.276/.326
2020	BAL	MLB	34	315	37	12	0	14	41	36	124	1	0	.206/.306/.403

Comparables: Ryan Howard, Carlos Pena, Jonny Gomes

There was a wraparound stretch across 2018 and 2019 during which Davis set a major-league record, going 62 consecutive plate appearances without a hit. Something like that doesn't happen without very bad luck, but striking out in 30 of those trips to the plate surely didn't help. Since he signed his miserable seven-year, $161 million contract ahead of the 2016 season, 96 players have at least 2,000 plate appearances and Davis has the eighth-lowest soft contact rate among them. It's just that his 36.1 percent strikeout rate is miles ahead of anyone else, culminating in a 39.5 percent strikeout rate last season—another major-league record (min 350 PA) that he will wear. Another year and Davis will have been known as "Crush" longer for his impact on the Orioles' payroll than on opposing pitchers' fastballs.

YEAR	TEAM	LVL	AGE	PA	DRC+	VORP	BABIP	BRR	FRAA	WARP
2017	BAL	MLB	31	524	88	-1.4	.301	-2.0	1B(125): 4.2, 3B(2): -0.1	0.2
2018	BAL	MLB	32	522	56	-28.7	.237	-4.6	1B(116): -5.4	-3.2
2019	BAL	MLB	33	352	65	-1.6	.270	0.7	1B(97): -4.6, P(1): 0.0	-1.5
2020	BAL	MLB	34	315	84	-2.7	.311	-1.1	1B -2	-0.4

Chris Davis, continued

Batted Ball Distribution

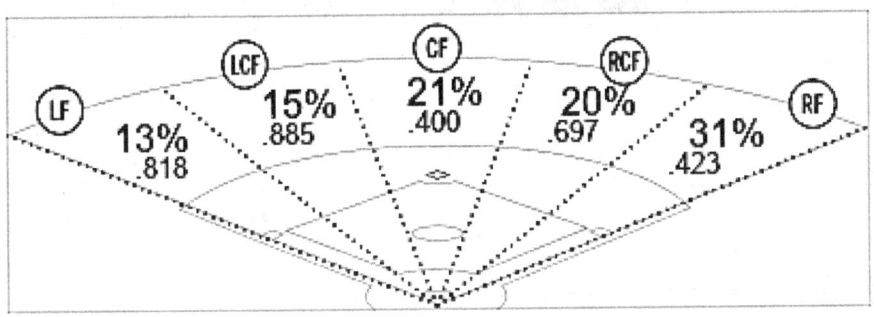

Strike Zone vs LHP   **Strike Zone vs RHP**

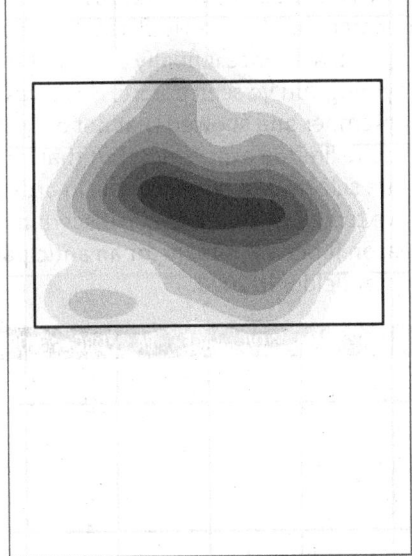

Baltimore Orioles 2020

Austin Hays CF
Born: 07/05/95   Age: 24   Bats: R   Throws: R
Height: 6'1"   Weight: 195   Origin: Round 3, 2016 Draft (#91 overall)

YEAR	TEAM	LVL	AGE	PA	R	2B	3B	HR	RBI	BB	K	SB	CS	AVG/OBP/SLG
2017	FRD	A+	21	280	42	15	3	16	41	12	40	4	6	.328/.364/.592
2017	BOW	AA	21	283	39	17	2	16	54	13	45	1	1	.330/.367/.594
2017	BAL	MLB	21	63	4	3	0	1	8	2	16	0	0	.217/.238/.317
2018	ABE	A-	22	39	6	2	0	0	3	2	7	0	0	.189/.231/.243
2018	BOW	AA	22	288	34	12	2	12	43	12	59	6	3	.242/.271/.432
2019	FRD	A+	23	40	3	0	0	2	6	1	11	0	0	.162/.200/.324
2019	BOW	AA	23	61	9	5	0	3	11	5	11	3	1	.268/.328/.518
2019	NOR	AAA	23	257	43	16	1	10	27	11	61	6	4	.254/.304/.454
2019	BAL	MLB	23	75	12	6	0	4	13	7	13	2	0	.309/.373/.574
2020	BAL	MLB	24	350	43	19	1	19	54	16	85	2	1	.253/.293/.490

Comparables: Christian Yelich, Nomar Mazara, Tyler Colvin

Since Hays became the first 2016 draftee to make his debut in September 2017, his career has been a Netflix series where you just keep waiting for something to happen. And once it finally does at the end, it doesn't really connect with anything you've seen before. Hays was summoned to the majors again last September and showed that not only can he play an impressive center field despite limited experience, but that he took the organization's advice to be more selective to heart as well. In order for the new approach to work, Hays will have to figure out how to be discerning without becoming too passive, but his season finale set him up for an anticipated premiere as the Orioles' presumptive center fielder in 2020.

YEAR	TEAM	LVL	AGE	PA	DRC+	VORP	BABIP	BRR	FRAA	WARP
2017	FRD	A+	21	280	149	25.5	.337	0.7	CF(57): 8.1, RF(4): -0.6	3.1
2017	BOW	AA	21	283	157	31.3	.345	3.2	CF(32): -3.3, RF(29): -0.4	2.4
2017	BAL	MLB	21	63	70	-3.3	.273	-0.4	RF(14): -1.6, CF(8): -1.3	-0.4
2018	ABE	A-	22	39	92	-2.9	.233	0.0	RF(5): -0.6	0.0
2018	BOW	AA	22	288	89	8.3	.263	0.9	RF(36): 6.7, LF(16): -0.3	1.1
2019	FRD	A+	23	40	41	-1.0	.160	0.2	CF(7): -0.7	-0.2
2019	BOW	AA	23	61	142	3.2	.286	-1.1	RF(7): 1.2, CF(4): 0.0	0.4
2019	NOR	AAA	23	257	93	10.1	.302	4.2	CF(38): 4.8, RF(16): 0.0	1.3
2019	BAL	MLB	23	75	111	3.9	.333	0.8	CF(20): 2.3	0.7
2020	BAL	MLB	24	350	98	11.9	.283	-0.4	CF 4	1.6

Austin Hays, continued

Batted Ball Distribution

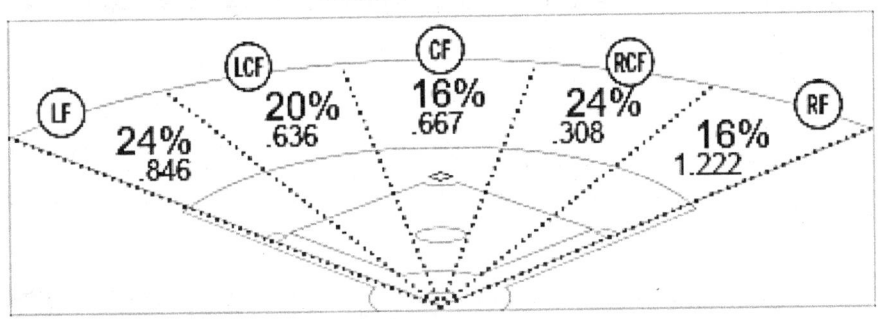

Strike Zone vs LHP   Strike Zone vs RHP

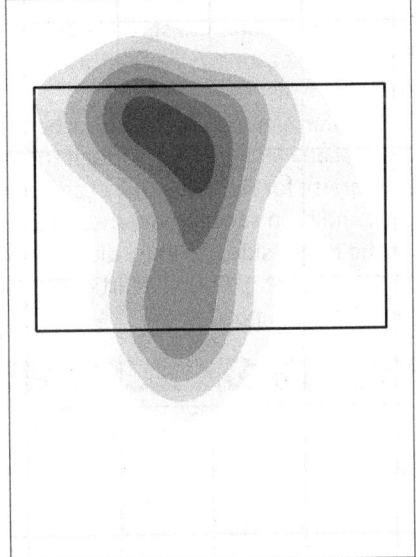

Baltimore Orioles 2020

Bryan Holaday C
Born: 11/19/87   Age: 32   Bats: R   Throws: R
Height: 6'0"   Weight: 214   Origin: Round 6, 2010 Draft (#193 overall)

YEAR	TEAM	LVL	AGE	PA	R	2B	3B	HR	RBI	BB	K	SB	CS	AVG/OBP/SLG
2017	TOL	AAA	29	347	31	20	0	12	50	22	54	0	3	.269/.325/.450
2017	DET	MLB	29	29	1	2	0	0	2	0	1	0	0	.241/.241/.310
2018	MIA	MLB	30	166	7	5	0	1	16	10	29	0	0	.205/.261/.258
2019	NWO	AAA	31	118	8	7	0	2	12	17	12	1	1	.247/.385/.387
2019	MIA	MLB	31	129	12	6	0	4	12	11	21	0	1	.278/.344/.435
2020	MIA	MLB	32	251	23	11	0	6	25	17	48	1	0	.222/.288/.352

Comparables: Robert Machado, Brian Johnson, Yorvit Torrealba

YEAR	TEAM	P. COUNT	FRM RUNS	BLK RUNS	THRW RUNS	TOT RUNS
2017	DET	1073	-1.4	-1.4	0.0	-3.0
2017	TOL	12913	-3.0	3.9	2.5	2.7
2018	MIA	6233	2.8	0.9	0.4	4.0
2019	MIA	5153	-4.8	-0.1	0.0	-4.9
2019	NWO	4286	3.4	0.0	0.6	3.8
2020	MIA	12365	-9.0	-1.1	-0.3	-10.5

It's a luxury to have a backup catcher who can make some noise with the stick, and it's a downright excess for a cellar dweller like the Marlins to have enjoyed Holaday's 2019 season. After 600 plate appearances spread over his first seven seasons, Holaday "broke out" at the dish while backing up Jorge Alfaro, managing the third-best DRC+ of any Miami hitter, though that itself is more an indictment of the Marlins than praise for Holaday. Unfortunately, he swallowed those gains—giving it all back and then some on defense by being one of the league's 10 worst framers. On the bright side, Holaday did lower his career ERA to 7.36 after getting fellow backup backstop Russell Martin to ground out to end a meaningless 15-1 drubbing in August.

YEAR	TEAM	LVL	AGE	PA	DRC+	VORP	BABIP	BRR	FRAA	WARP
2017	TOL	AAA	29	347	107	18.7	.286	-3.2	C(90): 3.8, 3B(3): 0.0	1.9
2017	DET	MLB	29	29	87	-1.2	.250	0.5	C(11): -2.9, 2B(1): 0.0	-0.1
2018	MIA	MLB	30	166	81	-4.9	.244	-1.5	C(50): 4.5, P(2): 0.0	0.7
2019	NWO	AAA	31	118	108	8.2	.259	0.5	C(34): 4.1	1.1
2019	MIA	MLB	31	129	97	6.3	.308	-2.3	C(38): -5.2, P(1): 0.0	-0.1
2020	MIA	MLB	32	251	71	-2.6	.257	-1.2	C -10, 3B 0	-1.3

Bryan Holaday, continued

Batted Ball Distribution

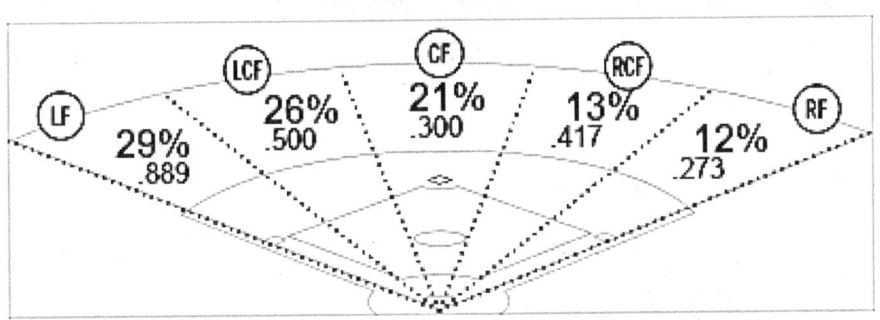

Strike Zone vs LHP   Strike Zone vs RHP

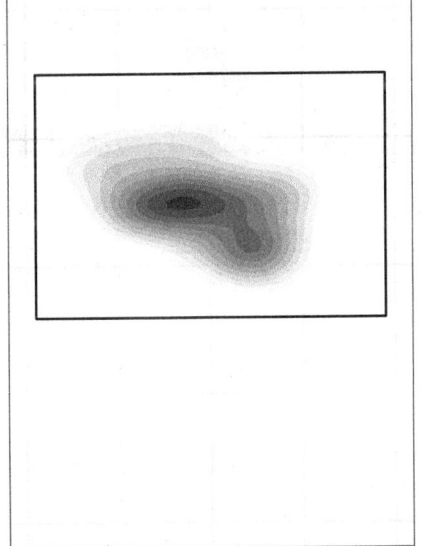

Orioles Player Analysis - 27

Baltimore Orioles 2020

José Iglesias SS

Born: 01/05/90 Age: 30 Bats: R Throws: R
Height: 5'11" Weight: 194 Origin: International Free Agent, 2009

YEAR	TEAM	LVL	AGE	PA	R	2B	3B	HR	RBI	BB	K	SB	CS	AVG/OBP/SLG
2017	DET	MLB	27	489	56	33	1	6	54	21	65	7	4	.255/.288/.369
2018	DET	MLB	28	464	43	31	3	5	48	19	47	15	6	.269/.310/.389
2019	CIN	MLB	29	530	62	21	3	11	59	20	70	6	6	.288/.318/.407
2020	BAL	MLB	30	525	49	25	1	10	52	24	69	10	5	.265/.306/.379

Comparables: Jean Segura, Erick Aybar, Angel Berroa

If it feels like Iglesias has been around forever, it's because he has—he's an immortal shapeshifter who has taken many faces and names over the years. No, no, we're just kidding about that ... it's because he first debuted on the 2011 Red Sox, a team that featured Kevin Youkilis, Daisuke Matsuzaka and Mike Cameron, among others. And yet Iglesias will play this season at the ripe age of 30 following a solid season in 2019 that saw him slug over .400 for the first time in his career. He remains a plus defensive shortstop, but one interesting change within his profile is that he's increased his swing rate to career-high levels in each of the past three seasons. Walking was never something Iglesias cared to do, so we applaud him leaning into it.

YEAR	TEAM	LVL	AGE	PA	DRC+	VORP	BABIP	BRR	FRAA	WARP
2017	DET	MLB	27	489	72	4.8	.285	3.7	SS(130): -4.8	0.4
2018	DET	MLB	28	464	93	18.0	.291	1.6	SS(122): 4.7	2.3
2019	CIN	MLB	29	530	86	16.2	.315	3.0	SS(144): 6.5	2.5
2020	BAL	MLB	30	525	79	8.3	.292	2.5	SS 2	1.1

José Iglesias, continued

Batted Ball Distribution

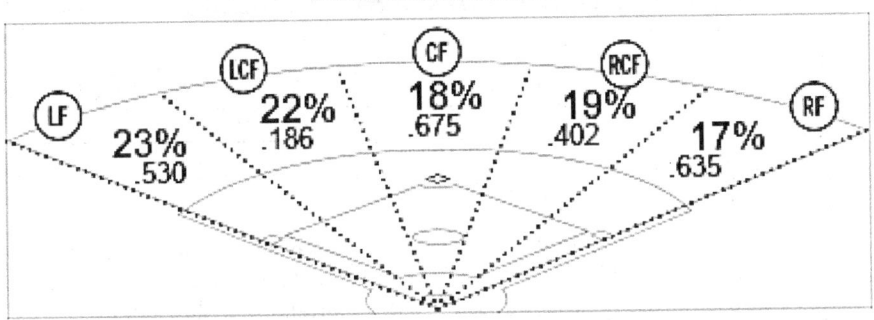

Strike Zone vs LHP   **Strike Zone vs RHP**

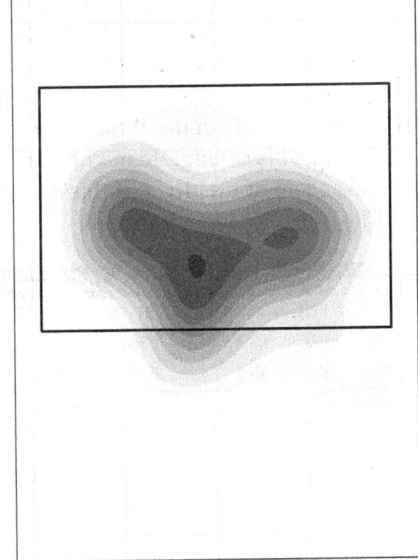

Baltimore Orioles 2020

Trey Mancini OF/1B
Born: 03/18/92 Age: 28 Bats: R Throws: R
Height: 6'4" Weight: 215 Origin: Round 8, 2013 Draft (#249 overall)

YEAR	TEAM	LVL	AGE	PA	R	2B	3B	HR	RBI	BB	K	SB	CS	AVG/OBP/SLG
2017	BAL	MLB	25	586	65	26	4	24	78	33	139	1	0	.293/.338/.488
2018	BAL	MLB	26	636	69	23	3	24	58	44	153	0	1	.242/.299/.416
2019	BAL	MLB	27	679	106	38	2	35	97	63	143	1	0	.291/.364/.535
2020	BAL	MLB	28	525	71	25	2	29	83	42	115	1	0	.277/.342/.519

Comparables: Brant Brown, Rico Brogna, Mitch Moreland

There's a bit of a misnomer about Mancini around Baltimore that he's a young player still, but at age 27, he's finally hitting arbitration around the time that actual young stars are nearing free agency. No matter. Put a player of his experience as the only legitimate threat in a lineup made to lose 100 games, and all you can ask is he takes as many steps forward as Mancini did in 2019. He was among the most productive outfielders in the American League, and all of it was backed up by legitimate underlying improvements from his inconsistent 2018. If you could pick any three stats for a power hitter to improve, it would be raising his walk rate and lowering both his strikeout and groundball rates—and Mancini did all three. So, despite no opposing pitcher having any real reason to pitch to him, Mancini still got his. While he was jobbed a bit in not being an All-Star in 2019, that's his ceiling. He might be miscast as a franchise face, and definitely is miscast as an outfielder, but this is a player who is capable of hitting in the middle of any order in baseball.

YEAR	TEAM	LVL	AGE	PA	DRC+	VORP	BABIP	BRR	FRAA	WARP
2017	BAL	MLB	25	586	106	22.6	.352	0.9	LF(88): 0.9, 1B(45): -2.1	1.6
2018	BAL	MLB	26	636	92	2.5	.285	0.5	LF(98): 4.5, 1B(47): 2.7	1.5
2019	BAL	MLB	27	679	120	31.8	.326	-0.9	RF(87): -3.6, 1B(56): 1.7	2.8
2020	BAL	MLB	28	525	119	23.5	.310	0.2	1B 0, RF -1	2.4

Trey Mancini, continued

Batted Ball Distribution

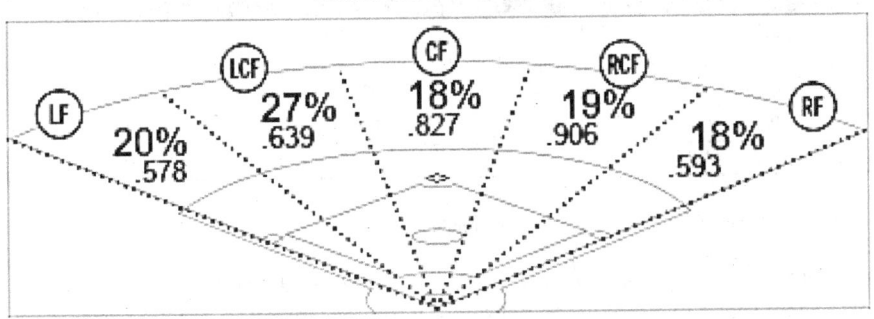

Strike Zone vs LHP   **Strike Zone vs RHP**

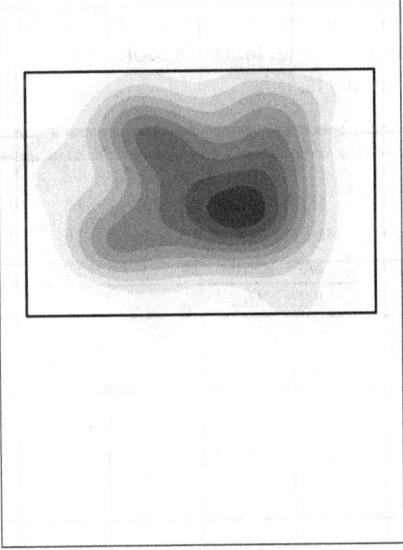

Baltimore Orioles 2020

Richie Martin SS

Born: 12/22/94   Age: 25   Bats: R   Throws: R
Height: 5'11"   Weight: 190   Origin: Round 1, 2015 Draft (#20 overall)

YEAR	TEAM	LVL	AGE	PA	R	2B	3B	HR	RBI	BB	K	SB	CS	AVG/OBP/SLG
2017	STO	A+	22	103	16	2	3	1	6	8	21	1	1	.266/.330/.383
2017	MID	AA	22	325	43	11	3	3	27	24	57	12	3	.224/.306/.315
2018	MID	AA	23	509	68	29	8	6	42	44	86	25	10	.300/.368/.439
2019	BAL	MLB	24	309	29	8	3	6	23	14	83	10	1	.208/.260/.322
2020	BAL	MLB	25	70	6	3	0	1	7	4	19	1	1	.212/.274/.329

Comparables: Danny Worth, Yadiel Rivera, Erick Mejia

Even if there's an extremely low bar for success when the subject is a Rule 5 pick on a team that's just looking to get talent in the organization, Martin's rookie year could not have been less conclusive. He hit well enough in the second half, but really only against lefties. He looked the part at shortstop, but the team combats the public-facing metrics that don't flatter him by saying their internal ones rate him well. The overall package of a speedy infielder who can lay down a bunt, make all the plays at shortstop and literally run into an extra-base hit is a valuable one. Martin's rookie season just didn't make it clear that's what he actually is.

YEAR	TEAM	LVL	AGE	PA	DRC+	VORP	BABIP	BRR	FRAA	WARP
2017	STO	A+	22	103	98	3.3	.333	0.0	SS(14): 0.3	0.3
2017	MID	AA	22	325	64	9.0	.266	3.3	SS(86): -8.2	-0.2
2018	MID	AA	23	509	120	28.4	.357	-0.3	SS(96): 9.1, 2B(21): 1.0	4.1
2019	BAL	MLB	24	309	50	-5.2	.272	-0.9	SS(117): -0.8	-0.7
2020	BAL	MLB	25	70	60	-1.3	.278	-0.3	SS 0	-0.2

Richie Martin, *continued*

Batted Ball Distribution

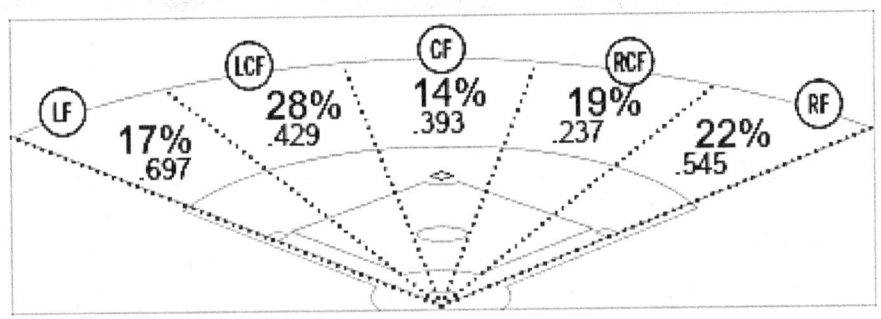

Strike Zone vs LHP   **Strike Zone vs RHP**

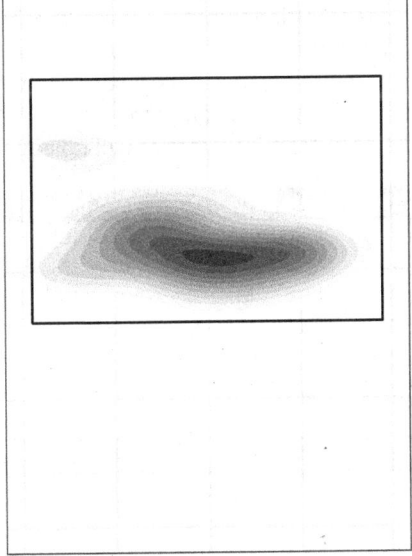

Baltimore Orioles 2020

Cedric Mullins CF
Born: 10/01/94 Age: 25 Bats: B Throws: L
Height: 5'8" Weight: 175 Origin: Round 13, 2015 Draft (#403 overall)

YEAR	TEAM	LVL	AGE	PA	R	2B	3B	HR	RBI	BB	K	SB	CS	AVG/OBP/SLG
2017	BOW	AA	22	350	53	19	1	13	37	27	58	9	7	.265/.319/.460
2018	BOW	AA	23	218	36	12	5	6	28	15	28	9	1	.313/.362/.512
2018	NOR	AAA	23	269	41	17	3	6	19	22	39	12	0	.269/.333/.438
2018	BAL	MLB	23	191	23	9	0	4	11	17	37	2	3	.235/.312/.359
2019	BOW	AA	24	226	35	11	0	5	18	22	31	20	3	.271/.341/.402
2019	NOR	AAA	24	306	40	8	2	5	24	25	51	13	4	.205/.272/.306
2019	BAL	MLB	24	74	7	0	2	0	4	4	14	1	0	.094/.181/.156
2020	BAL	MLB	25	210	20	10	1	6	23	15	44	5	2	.222/.281/.379

Comparables: Mallex Smith, Gary Geiger, Oddibe McDowell

When the Orioles worried near the end of the Adam Jones era that replacing him in center field would be a tougher task on the field than off it, even the most cynical couldn't envision Mullins being demoted to Double-A while trying. Conan O'Brien thinks his run at the Tonight Show went well by comparison. That return to Double-A Bowie for the North Carolina native seemed to allow him to not only reset as a player, but reset expectations. Maybe now, a speedy slasher type who can patrol center field but tops out as a bench outfielder will be an outcome all parties will take.

YEAR	TEAM	LVL	AGE	PA	DRC+	VORP	BABIP	BRR	FRAA	WARP
2017	BOW	AA	22	350	101	15.6	.283	0.9	CF(57): 7.2, LF(8): 1.1	2.0
2018	BOW	AA	23	218	136	22.8	.339	2.4	CF(43): 0.4, LF(3): 0.5	1.8
2018	NOR	AAA	23	269	122	15.0	.298	2.2	CF(60): 0.2	1.7
2018	BAL	MLB	23	191	82	1.6	.279	-0.6	CF(45): -3.8, LF(1): 0.0	-0.2
2019	BOW	AA	24	226	127	16.5	.293	2.8	CF(30): 0.9, LF(19): 0.1	1.7
2019	NOR	AAA	24	306	50	-9.3	.231	1.8	CF(56): 4.1, LF(6): -0.6	-0.3
2019	BAL	MLB	24	74	57	-1.5	.118	0.5	CF(22): 1.4	0.0
2020	BAL	MLB	25	210	69	-0.5	.258	0.3	CF 3	0.2

Cedric Mullins, continued

Batted Ball Distribution

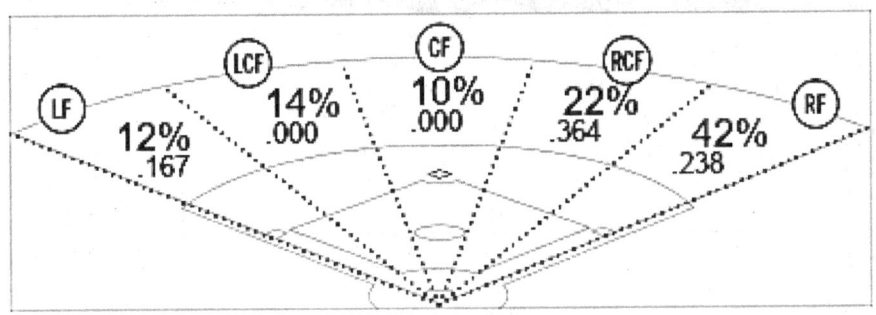

Strike Zone vs LHP   Strike Zone vs RHP

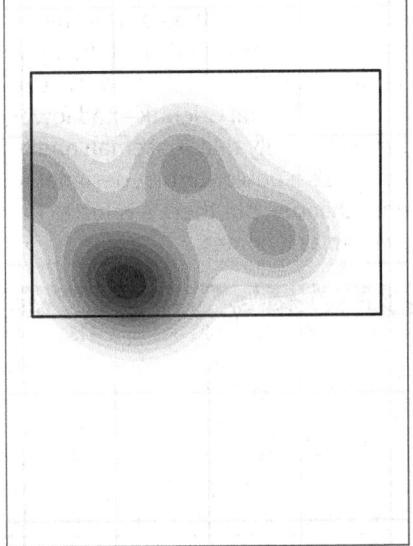

Baltimore Orioles 2020

Renato Núñez DH

Born: 04/04/94 Age: 26 Bats: R Throws: R
Height: 6'1" Weight: 220 Origin: International Free Agent, 2010

YEAR	TEAM	LVL	AGE	PA	R	2B	3B	HR	RBI	BB	K	SB	CS	AVG/OBP/SLG
2017	NAS	AAA	23	533	74	27	2	32	78	47	141	2	1	.249/.319/.518
2017	OAK	MLB	23	16	1	0	0	1	3	1	8	0	0	.200/.250/.400
2018	NAS	AAA	24	30	3	0	0	0	4	2	6	0	0	.357/.400/.357
2018	NOR	AAA	24	228	25	14	1	5	25	23	49	1	0	.289/.361/.443
2018	TEX	MLB	24	41	2	1	0	1	2	3	12	0	0	.167/.244/.278
2018	BAL	MLB	24	220	26	13	0	7	20	16	50	0	0	.275/.336/.445
2019	BAL	MLB	25	599	72	24	0	31	90	44	143	1	1	.244/.311/.460
2020	BAL	MLB	26	525	66	20	1	29	79	37	131	1	0	.241/.305/.468

Comparables: Wilson Betemit, Michael Cuddyer, Adrián González

Summoned from the minors to take over as the Orioles' everyday third baseman after they traded Manny Machado, Núñez coming to Baltimore was modern-day baseball equivalent of replacing Vin Diesel in the Fast franchise with Billy Zane because they're both bald. The shine they share in a baseball sense is raw power in games (and nice smiles off them), with Núñez being one of 61 players to reach the 30-homer plateau this season. Only three of them—Rougned Odor, José Abreu and Randal Grichuk—had lower a WARP than Núñez, who became an emergency-only third baseman and is far down the Orioles' first base depth chart. He's a power-hitting designated hitter in an era when power has never come cheaper, but there's value to the Orioles as long as that power is literally as cheap as it comes.

YEAR	TEAM	LVL	AGE	PA	DRC+	VORP	BABIP	BRR	FRAA	WARP
2017	NAS	AAA	23	533	113	24.5	.279	-1.5	LF(48): -7.0, 3B(44): -4.7	0.9
2017	OAK	MLB	23	16	70	-0.5	.333	-0.2	LF(3): -0.2, 3B(1): 0.2	0.0
2018	NAS	AAA	24	30	101	1.4	.455	-0.5	3B(2): -0.2, LF(2): -0.5	0.0
2018	NOR	AAA	24	228	134	12.2	.356	0.8	3B(38): 0.1, 1B(6): 0.6	1.6
2018	TEX	MLB	24	41	94	-0.8	.208	-0.2	3B(8): 0.9, LF(4): -0.2	0.2
2018	BAL	MLB	24	220	95	8.4	.333	-0.8	3B(59): -4.0	0.2
2019	BAL	MLB	25	599	99	9.8	.272	-2.1	1B(24): -1.9, 3B(9): 0.0	0.6
2020	BAL	MLB	26	525	95	2.0	.270	-1.3	3B 0, 1B 0	0.2

Renato Núñez, continued

Batted Ball Distribution

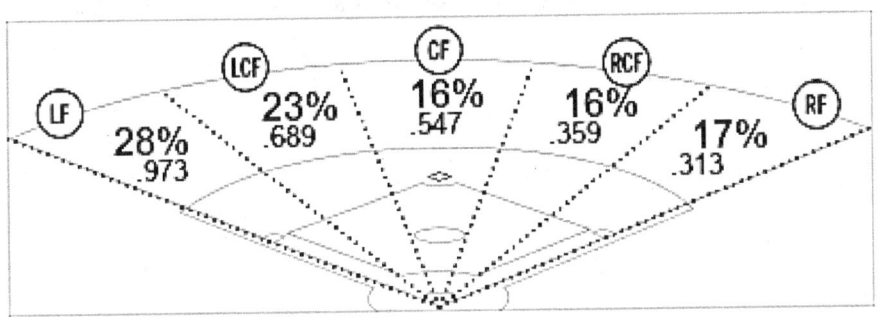

Strike Zone vs LHP

Strike Zone vs RHP

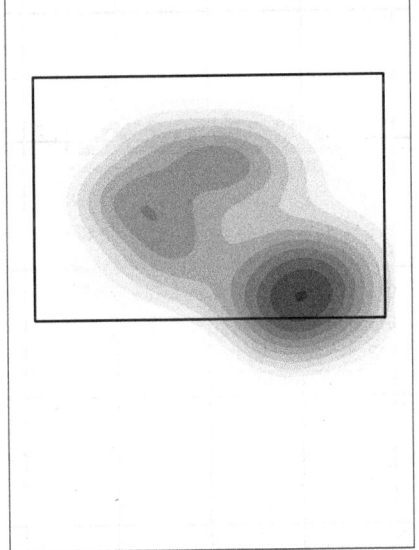

Baltimore Orioles 2020

José Rondón INF

Born: 03/03/94 Age: 26 Bats: R Throws: R
Height: 6'1" Weight: 195 Origin: International Free Agent, 2011

YEAR	TEAM	LVL	AGE	PA	R	2B	3B	HR	RBI	BB	K	SB	CS	AVG/OBP/SLG
2017	SAN	AA	23	234	30	12	3	4	28	16	43	2	1	.293/.343/.433
2017	ELP	AAA	23	91	9	8	0	1	14	6	16	1	0	.282/.330/.412
2018	CHR	AAA	24	336	41	15	4	18	38	16	82	5	6	.249/.290/.495
2018	CHA	MLB	24	107	15	6	0	6	14	7	30	2	1	.230/.280/.470
2019	NOR	AAA	25	83	9	4	0	2	12	10	22	1	0	.219/.313/.356
2019	CHA	MLB	25	156	10	3	0	3	9	11	38	0	0	.197/.265/.282
2019	BAL	MLB	25	1	0	0	0	0	0	0	0	0	0	.000/.000/.000
2020	BAL	MLB	26	251	26	11	1	9	30	14	63	4	2	.232/.280/.397

Comparables: Roy Smalley, Johan Camargo, Yairo Muñoz

Before he can settle into his future role as a utility infielder for hire, the few days Rondón spent with the Orioles were typical of their 2019 season. He was run through his paces all over the outfield and, perhaps deemed unfit to be a makeshift outfielder, was sent down to the minors. Rondón could be in a large category of players kept from doing what they're best at by the Orioles' constant experimenting; it's just unclear what he's actually best at.

YEAR	TEAM	LVL	AGE	PA	DRC+	VORP	BABIP	BRR	FRAA	WARP
2017	SAN	AA	23	234	106	17.0	.349	1.4	SS(32): 4.4, 2B(11): -1.2	1.5
2017	ELP	AAA	23	91	89	2.9	.338	0.4	SS(18): 0.3, 2B(3): -0.3	0.3
2018	CHR	AAA	24	336	100	14.6	.278	0.9	SS(78): 10.9, 3B(2): 0.0	2.7
2018	CHA	MLB	24	107	94	2.3	.266	-1.0	SS(10): -0.4, 3B(8): 0.5	0.2
2019	NOR	AAA	25	83	87	1.3	.286	0.9	SS(14): 0.8, 3B(3): -0.2	0.3
2019	CHA	MLB	25	156	67	-0.6	.248	-0.8	2B(18): -0.1, SS(15): -1.3	-0.5
2019	BAL	MLB	25	1	185	0.1	.000	0.0	3B(1): 0.0	0.0
2020	BAL	MLB	26	251	76	-0.5	.281	-0.9	SS 3, 2B 0	0.3

José Rondón, continued

Batted Ball Distribution

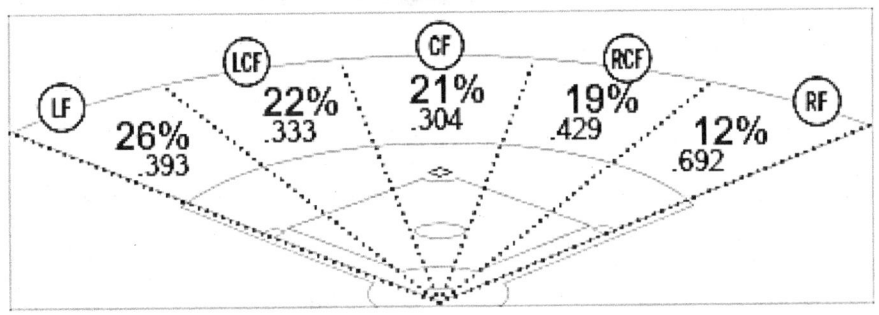

Strike Zone vs LHP   **Strike Zone vs RHP**

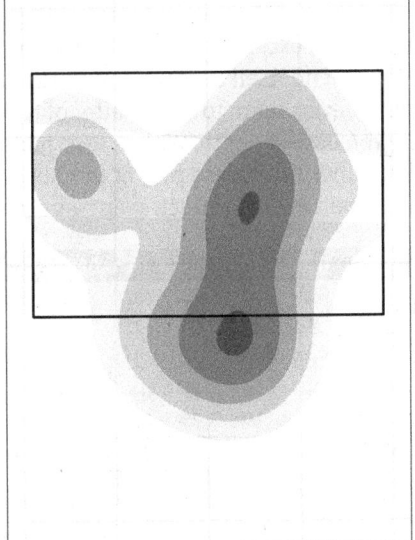

Rio Ruiz 3B

Born: 05/22/94 Age: 26 Bats: L Throws: R
Height: 6'1" Weight: 215 Origin: Round 4, 2012 Draft (#129 overall)

YEAR	TEAM	LVL	AGE	PA	R	2B	3B	HR	RBI	BB	K	SB	CS	AVG/OBP/SLG
2017	GWN	AAA	23	432	48	25	2	16	56	42	110	1	2	.247/.322/.446
2017	ATL	MLB	23	173	22	5	0	4	19	19	41	1	0	.193/.283/.307
2018	GWN	AAA	24	541	72	25	4	9	72	40	90	2	1	.269/.322/.390
2018	ATL	MLB	24	15	1	0	0	0	0	2	5	0	0	.083/.267/.083
2019	BAL	MLB	25	413	35	13	2	12	46	40	88	0	1	.232/.306/.376
2020	BAL	MLB	26	280	29	12	1	9	32	27	64	1	0	.232/.307/.392

Comparables: Lonnie Chisenhall, Andy Marte, Nicky Delmonico

Is Dad Strength a real thing? Consider the case of Ruiz, who spent a few weeks in the minors from late July into August that coincided with the birth of his son, Luca, and hit the O's only walk-off home run of the season against the Houston Astros (the team that drafted him) in his first start back. Ruiz hit seven home runs in 124 plate appearances following his August 10 return, after hitting nine in 484 career plate appearances leading up to that. There's literally nothing to explain it, except *perhaps* a better approach. His contact rates didn't change in a way to lend itself to more power. His exit velocity stayed flat most of the year. It didn't even seem to be a matter of luck. So, by process of elimination, it has to be the Dad Strength. With it, Ruiz had a .779 OPS and just enough pop to make his standout defense play at third base. Without it, he's a glove-first third baseman with too much swing-and-miss. And he's very much with it so far.

YEAR	TEAM	LVL	AGE	PA	DRC+	VORP	BABIP	BRR	FRAA	WARP
2017	GWN	AAA	23	432	116	13.2	.304	-0.2	3B(91): 2.0, 1B(5): 0.2	2.3
2017	ATL	MLB	23	173	76	-0.9	.231	0.9	3B(41): 0.6, 1B(2): 0.0	0.3
2018	GWN	AAA	24	541	96	9.9	.311	1.8	3B(49): 2.3, 1B(35): 1.5	1.2
2018	ATL	MLB	24	15	78	0.3	.143	-0.1	3B(1): -0.2	0.0
2019	BAL	MLB	25	413	81	5.3	.272	-1.4	3B(114): 2.3, 1B(12): 0.3	0.6
2020	BAL	MLB	26	280	80	-0.5	.276	-0.1	3B 1	0.0

Rio Ruiz, continued

Batted Ball Distribution

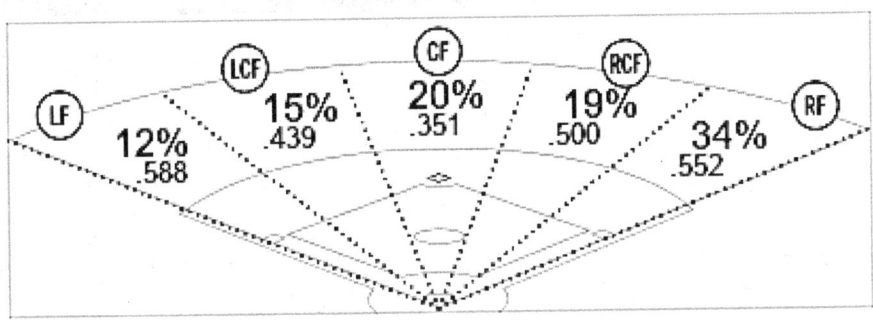

| Strike Zone vs LHP | Strike Zone vs RHP |

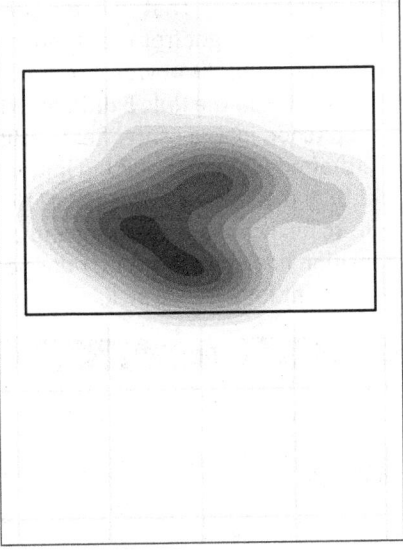

Baltimore Orioles 2020

Anthony Santander OF
Born: 10/19/94 Age: 25 Bats: B Throws: R
Height: 6'2" Weight: 190 Origin: International Free Agent, 2011

YEAR	TEAM	LVL	AGE	PA	R	2B	3B	HR	RBI	BB	K	SB	CS	AVG/OBP/SLG
2017	BOW	AA	22	59	13	5	0	5	14	7	9	0	0	.380/.458/.780
2017	BAL	MLB	22	31	1	3	0	0	2	0	8	0	0	.267/.258/.367
2018	ABE	A-	23	31	6	5	0	1	5	2	5	2	0	.286/.355/.571
2018	BOW	AA	23	222	26	9	3	5	22	10	32	4	1	.258/.293/.402
2018	NOR	AAA	23	47	3	3	0	2	7	2	9	0	0	.182/.213/.386
2018	BAL	MLB	23	108	8	5	1	1	6	6	21	1	0	.198/.250/.297
2019	NOR	AAA	24	209	30	15	0	5	28	13	38	3	2	.259/.311/.415
2019	BAL	MLB	24	405	46	20	1	20	59	19	86	1	2	.261/.297/.476
2020	BAL	MLB	25	525	59	29	1	23	72	27	120	3	1	.248/.293/.453

Comparables: Paul Householder, Jake Marisnick, Nomar Mazara

A front office with the Orioles' data-driven predilections operates under the assumption that they know what a player will become with enough minor-league experience. That said, the Orioles weren't banking on the kind of production they got from Santander when he was summoned from Triple-A Norfolk in June. His power showed through in a way it hadn't since 2016 - before he was taken in the Rule 5 draft and dealt with shoulder and elbow injuries - and even pitched in as a center fielder. His production only depreciated because he overdrafted his health and hid injuries in September, batting .155 in the final month of the season. Before that? He made a real statement, and showed the skills to be a capable defender and a useful bat off the bench if the Orioles ever transition back to being a first-division club. That's quite the return on investment for a Rule 5 pick.

YEAR	TEAM	LVL	AGE	PA	DRC+	VORP	BABIP	BRR	FRAA	WARP
2017	BOW	AA	22	59	193	8.4	.378	-0.7	RF(6): 0.0, LF(4): -0.2	0.6
2017	BAL	MLB	22	31	74	-0.1	.348	0.1	RF(8): 0.7, LF(4): -0.2	0.0
2018	ABE	A-	23	31	133	4.3	.318	0.2	RF(5): -0.2	0.1
2018	BOW	AA	23	222	87	4.8	.282	0.7	RF(35): -3.6, LF(14): -1.4	-0.3
2018	NOR	AAA	23	47	81	-1.7	.176	-0.1	RF(8): 1.1, LF(2): -0.3	0.1
2018	BAL	MLB	23	108	75	-5.9	.241	0.0	RF(29): 0.8, LF(1): 0.0	0.0
2019	NOR	AAA	24	209	85	-0.8	.298	1.1	RF(35): 1.8, LF(8): -0.9	0.2
2019	BAL	MLB	24	405	98	10.0	.285	-0.5	RF(50): -4.8, LF(40): 8.3	1.6
2020	BAL	MLB	25	525	86	3.7	.283	0.0	LF 10, RF 0	1.3

Anthony Santander, continued

Batted Ball Distribution

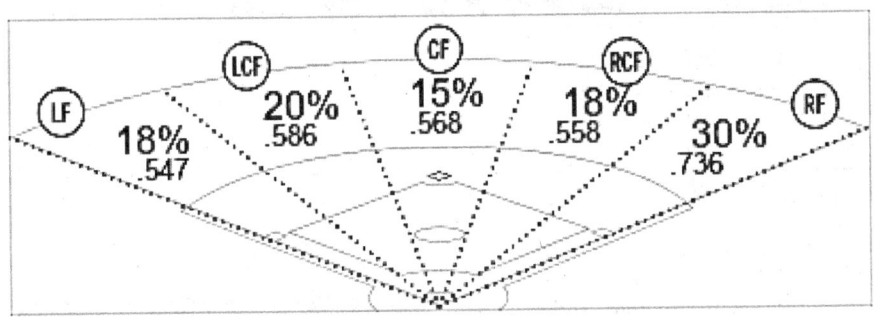

Strike Zone vs LHP   **Strike Zone vs RHP**

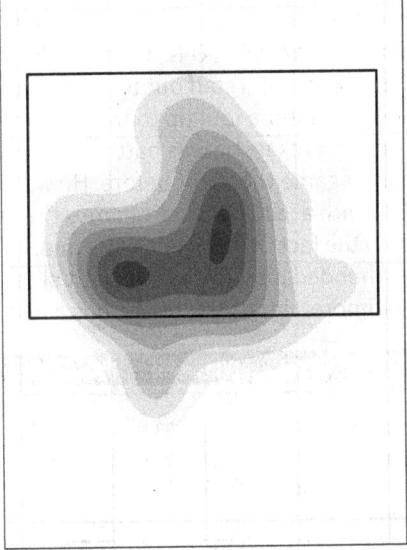

Baltimore Orioles 2020

Pedro Severino C

Born: 07/20/93 Age: 26 Bats: R Throws: R
Height: 6'1" Weight: 219 Origin: International Free Agent, 2010

YEAR	TEAM	LVL	AGE	PA	R	2B	3B	HR	RBI	BB	K	SB	CS	AVG/OBP/SLG
2017	SYR	AAA	23	227	17	4	0	5	29	15	43	1	1	.242/.291/.332
2017	WAS	MLB	23	31	0	1	0	0	3	2	10	0	0	.172/.226/.207
2018	SYR	AAA	24	136	14	5	1	6	13	5	23	0	0	.269/.294/.462
2018	WAS	MLB	24	213	14	9	0	2	15	18	47	1	0	.168/.254/.247
2019	BAL	MLB	25	341	37	13	0	13	44	29	73	3	1	.249/.321/.420
2020	BAL	MLB	26	315	33	12	0	11	38	22	67	1	1	.233/.293/.395

Comparables: Chris Snyder, Austin Hedges, Wilson Ramos

YEAR	TEAM	P. COUNT	FRM RUNS	BLK RUNS	THRW RUNS	TOT RUNS
2017	SYR	8269	8.1	-2.3	0.3	5.2
2017	WAS	939	0.7	-0.4	0.0	0.3
2018	SYR	4103	1.4	0.0	0.0	1.4
2018	WAS	8290	0.3	0.2	0.1	0.5
2019	BAL	12950	-9.6	-4.1	-0.2	-13.9
2020	BAL	12899	0.2	-1.2	-0.5	-1.5

Head injuries are no joke, and even if they're not specifically called concussions, they can be hidden inflection points in a player's season that explain what look like a sudden downturn in production. When home plate umpire Brian O'Nora called the Orioles' medical staff out to check on Severino after a foul tip to the face on June 5 in Texas, he was batting .286 with a .929 OPS, mostly thanks to a three-homer game the night before. He was back in the lineup two games later and hit .230 with a .640 OPS in 61 games the rest of the way. None of this takes away from the fact that Severino is a fine, if not often focused, defender who can hit left-handed pitching as the short side of a platoon but is asked to do far more in Baltimore. Here's hoping he has a restful offseason.

YEAR	TEAM	LVL	AGE	PA	DRC+	VORP	BABIP	BRR	FRAA	WARP
2017	SYR	AAA	23	227	86	3.1	.280	-0.4	C(58): 5.1	1.2
2017	WAS	MLB	23	31	60	-2.4	.263	-0.5	C(10): 0.3	0.0
2018	SYR	AAA	24	136	93	7.3	.284	-2.1	C(32): 1.1	0.4
2018	WAS	MLB	24	213	61	-6.9	.211	-0.1	C(67): 0.0	0.0
2019	BAL	MLB	25	341	91	13.3	.285	-2.4	C(89): -13.8	-0.3
2020	BAL	MLB	26	315	78	4.7	.266	-1.2	C -3	0.2

Pedro Severino, continued

Batted Ball Distribution

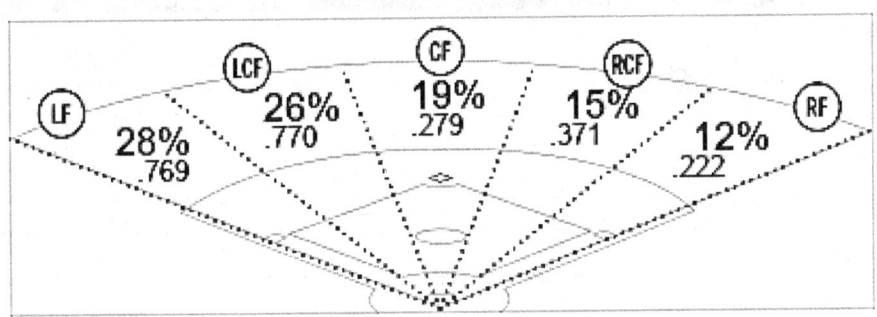

Strike Zone vs LHP   **Strike Zone vs RHP**

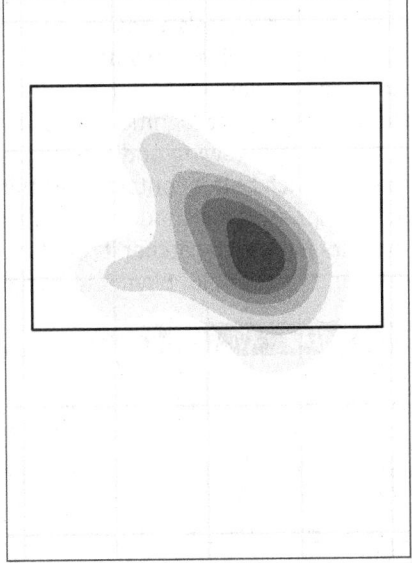

Baltimore Orioles 2020

Chance Sisco   C

Born: 02/24/95   Age: 25   Bats: L   Throws: R
Height: 6'2"   Weight: 195   Origin: Round 2, 2013 Draft (#61 overall)

YEAR	TEAM	LVL	AGE	PA	R	2B	3B	HR	RBI	BB	K	SB	CS	AVG/OBP/SLG
2017	NOR	AAA	22	388	47	23	0	7	47	32	99	2	2	.267/.340/.395
2017	BAL	MLB	22	22	3	2	0	2	4	3	7	0	0	.333/.455/.778
2018	NOR	AAA	23	151	22	5	0	3	12	16	36	0	0	.242/.344/.352
2018	BAL	MLB	23	184	13	8	0	2	16	13	66	1	0	.181/.288/.269
2019	NOR	AAA	24	196	31	10	0	10	37	20	44	0	0	.292/.388/.530
2019	BAL	MLB	24	198	29	7	0	8	20	22	61	0	1	.210/.333/.395
2020	BAL	MLB	25	315	35	13	0	11	38	29	91	1	0	.234/.325/.404

Comparables: Gary Sánchez, Dominic Smith, J.P. Crawford

There was a lot of risk in Sisco's profile coming up by virtue of his crude defensive skills and well-below average throwing arm, but as fate would have it, there's a possibility that the offensive profile that was supposed to mask over that is gone. He still has pitch recognition skills and cut down on his swing-and-miss while making much better contact in his third major-league season, though the all-fields approach that made him a top prospect is gone. There might be more room for a bat-first catcher if robots take over behind the plate, but sometimes you can't just wait for Skynet to take control.

YEAR	TEAM	P. COUNT	FRM RUNS	BLK RUNS	THRW RUNS	TOT RUNS
2017	BAL	653	-0.6	-0.2	-0.1	-1.1
2017	NOR	13196	5.9	1.1	-1.7	4.6
2018	BAL	6491	-2.2	0.3	-0.1	-2.1
2018	NOR	5151	-1.3	0.0	-0.8	-2.0
2019	BAL	6712	-9.6	-0.7	-0.5	-11.8
2019	NOR	4944	-1.8	0.3	-0.8	-2.5
2020	BAL	11846	-8.5	-0.6	-1.1	-10.1

YEAR	TEAM	LVL	AGE	PA	DRC+	VORP	BABIP	BRR	FRAA	WARP
2017	NOR	AAA	22	388	117	22.2	.351	1.9	C(94): 3.2	3.0
2017	BAL	MLB	22	22	94	3.8	.444	-0.3	C(10): -0.7	0.0
2018	NOR	AAA	23	151	114	5.4	.308	-1.1	C(37): -2.8	0.5
2018	BAL	MLB	23	184	58	-3.5	.293	-1.3	C(55): -2.8	-0.5
2019	NOR	AAA	24	196	131	16.8	.339	0.1	C(35): -3.3	1.2
2019	BAL	MLB	24	198	92	7.7	.276	0.1	C(52): -11.1, 1B(1): 0.0	-0.3
2020	BAL	MLB	25	315	90	10.1	.307	-0.5	C -11	-0.1

Chance Sisco, continued

Batted Ball Distribution

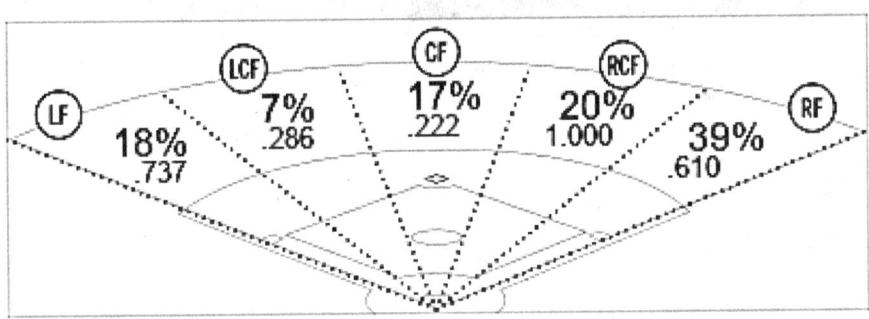

Strike Zone vs LHP   **Strike Zone vs RHP**

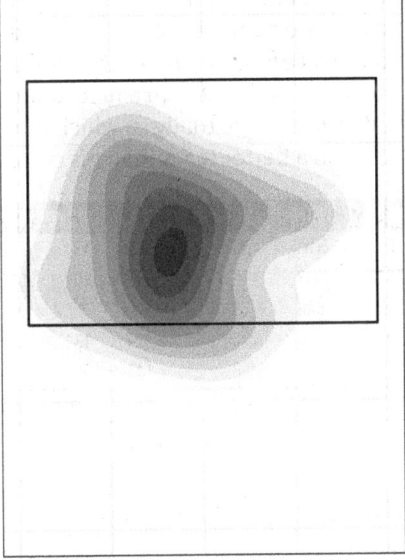

Orioles Player Analysis - 47

Baltimore Orioles 2020

DJ Stewart OF
Born: 11/30/93 Age: 26 Bats: L Throws: R
Height: 6'0" Weight: 230 Origin: Round 1, 2015 Draft (#25 overall)

YEAR	TEAM	LVL	AGE	PA	R	2B	3B	HR	RBI	BB	K	SB	CS	AVG/OBP/SLG
2017	BOW	AA	23	540	80	26	2	21	79	65	87	20	4	.278/.378/.481
2018	NOR	AAA	24	490	59	24	2	12	55	54	103	11	4	.235/.329/.387
2018	BAL	MLB	24	47	8	3	0	3	10	4	12	2	1	.250/.340/.550
2019	NOR	AAA	25	277	42	19	2	12	47	38	51	5	4	.291/.396/.548
2019	BAL	MLB	25	142	15	6	0	4	15	14	26	1	2	.238/.317/.381
2020	BAL	MLB	26	455	54	20	1	19	59	46	101	9	3	.229/.317/.425

Comparables: Alex Hassan, Preston Tucker, Nicky Delmonico

First-round picks are fun to have, but the wrong kind can be like a talented band that gets radio play early and has the fanbase they're trying to play for resent them for it. Enter Stewart, the Orioles' top pick in 2015. If he was a senior-sign who: played a reckless outfield to his own detriment; never saw a ball he didn't think he could hit or a throw he didn't think he could make; could work a walk and run into some power, even if it's a one-plane swing; who has won all his life, and wasn't afraid to swipe a base? He'd be every scout's sneaky favorite.
Instead, he's all that with a first-rounder's mentality and expectations. It doesn't change what he actually is, which is a corner bat with an approach and a bench profile on a better team than his current one.

YEAR	TEAM	LVL	AGE	PA	DRC+	VORP	BABIP	BRR	FRAA	WARP
2017	BOW	AA	23	540	134	37.2	.299	2.1	LF(113): -0.6, RF(4): 0.7	3.5
2018	NOR	AAA	24	490	107	14.3	.278	4.7	RF(88): -14.1, LF(24): 1.9	0.5
2018	BAL	MLB	24	47	88	3.2	.269	0.5	LF(9): 4.4, RF(6): -0.4	0.5
2019	NOR	AAA	25	277	131	18.6	.324	-2.1	LF(30): -1.2, RF(22): 1.6	1.4
2019	BAL	MLB	25	142	84	0.4	.268	-0.3	RF(26): -1.8, LF(11): -0.5	-0.2
2020	BAL	MLB	26	455	91	3.9	.258	-0.2	RF -9	-0.6

DJ Stewart, continued

Batted Ball Distribution

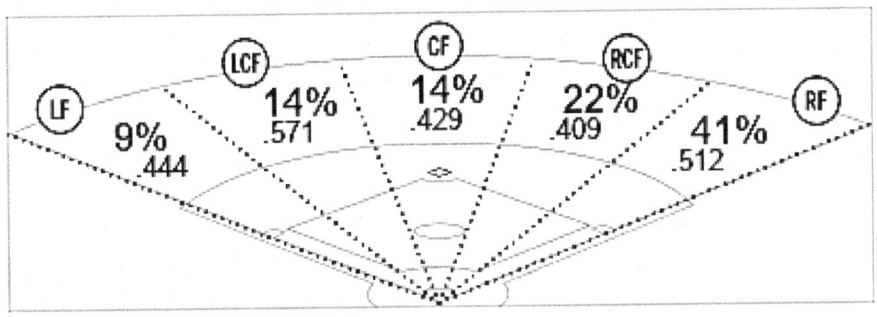

Strike Zone vs LHP   **Strike Zone vs RHP**

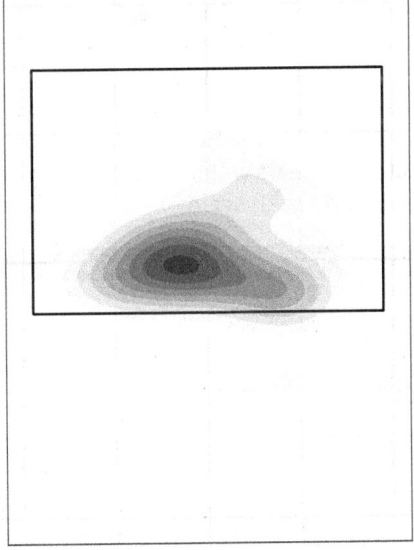

Baltimore Orioles 2020

Jesús Sucre C

Born: 04/30/88 Age: 32 Bats: R Throws: R
Height: 6'0" Weight: 200 Origin: International Free Agent, 2005

YEAR	TEAM	LVL	AGE	PA	R	2B	3B	HR	RBI	BB	K	SB	CS	AVG/OBP/SLG
2017	TBA	MLB	29	192	20	6	0	7	29	7	35	2	0	.256/.289/.409
2018	TBA	MLB	30	198	9	5	0	1	17	9	29	1	0	.209/.247/.253
2019	NOR	AAA	31	198	20	15	0	0	19	12	29	0	0	.283/.333/.364
2019	BAL	MLB	31	67	3	2	0	0	3	4	13	0	0	.210/.269/.242
2020	BAL	MLB	32	251	20	10	0	4	22	12	48	1	0	.221/.264/.316

Comparables: Pete Daley, Greg Myers, Pat Borders

Sucre might not have survived a season of catching this Orioles' pitching staff, so it's probably best that he didn't get the chance. A well-respected defender who throws out runners at an above-average clip and knows how to call a game, Sucre barely made it to April before every opposing home run he watched fly off the bat brought out a visceral—and visible—reaction of disgust. But if the Orioles' new front office could watch after being used to the Houston Astros' stellar arms, Sucre could have sucked it up after two years with the Tampa Bay Rays. Instead, he was outrighted before May and never seen again.

YEAR	TEAM	P. COUNT	FRM RUNS	BLK RUNS	THRW RUNS	TOT RUNS
2017	TBA	7812	4.1	0.9	-0.4	5.7
2018	TBA	7931	-4.9	0.7	0.0	-3.8
2019	BAL	2494	-0.9	-0.4	0.1	-1.1
2019	NOR	5325	-3.6	0.0	0.9	-2.7
2020	BAL	10097	0.0	0.1	1.5	1.6

YEAR	TEAM	LVL	AGE	PA	DRC+	VORP	BABIP	BRR	FRAA	WARP
2017	TBA	MLB	29	192	93	6.8	.275	0.2	C(61): 3.1, P(1): 0.0	1.1
2018	TBA	MLB	30	198	73	-9.1	.240	-1.8	C(71): -4.2, P(2): 0.0	-0.3
2019	NOR	AAA	31	198	101	0.6	.335	0.2	C(37): -3.8, 1B(2): 0.2	0.5
2019	BAL	MLB	31	67	78	1.5	.265	0.1	C(18): -1.1, P(1): 0.0	0.0
2020	BAL	MLB	32	251	54	-7.8	.263	-0.6	C 0, 1B 0	-0.8

Jesús Sucre, continued

Batted Ball Distribution

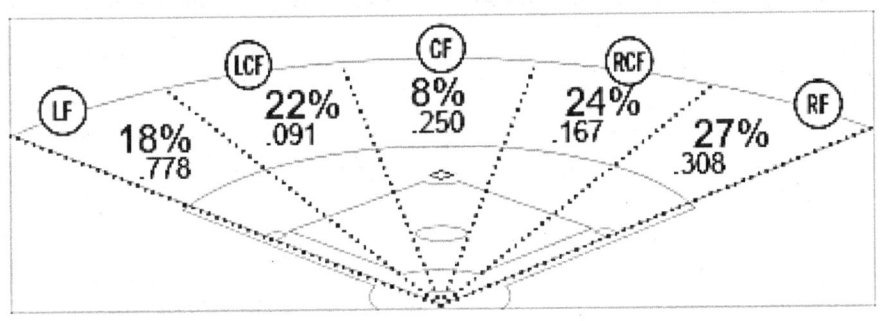

Strike Zone vs LHP   **Strike Zone vs RHP**

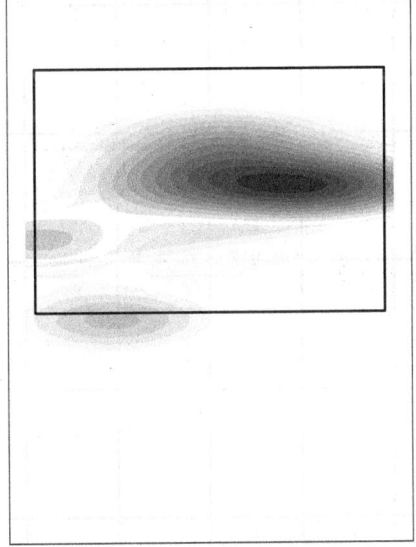

Baltimore Orioles 2020

Mark Trumbo DH

Born: 01/16/86   Age: 34   Bats: R   Throws: R
Height: 6'4"   Weight: 225   Origin: Round 18, 2004 Draft (#533 overall)

YEAR	TEAM	LVL	AGE	PA	R	2B	3B	HR	RBI	BB	K	SB	CS	AVG/OBP/SLG
2017	BAL	MLB	31	603	79	22	0	23	65	42	149	1	0	.234/.289/.397
2018	BAL	MLB	32	358	41	12	0	17	44	24	87	0	0	.261/.313/.452
2019	NOR	AAA	33	48	5	3	0	4	10	6	15	0	0	.214/.313/.571
2019	BAL	MLB	33	31	1	3	0	0	3	2	5	0	0	.172/.226/.276
2020	BAL	MLB	34	251	28	11	0	11	33	19	71	0	0	.230/.290/.422

Comparables: Dick Stuart, David Ortiz, Adrián González

Trumbo was somewhat unfairly moved to the outfield when Chris Davis was re-signed in 2016 and hit 47 home runs to lead the majors anyway. He was then unfairly lumped in with that disastrous $161-million Davis contract when he never matched that 2016 production over his own three-year, $37.5 million pact that concluded after 2019. He was duty-bound by that contract to come back in September after a complicated cartilage replacement surgery in his knee, the same that has ruined Dustin Pedroia's career. He did it, and wasn't himself. Here's hoping wherever he ends up in his future isn't close enough to Davis to remain in his gravitational pull.

YEAR	TEAM	LVL	AGE	PA	DRC+	VORP	BABIP	BRR	FRAA	WARP
2017	BAL	MLB	31	603	87	-8.4	.278	-2.3	RF(31): -4.6, 3B(2): 0.0	-0.7
2018	BAL	MLB	32	358	102	6.2	.303	0.9	RF(19): -1.4, 1B(3): 0.2	0.6
2019	NOR	AAA	33	48	121	2.3	.217	0.0	RF(2): -0.3, 1B(1): 0.0	0.2
2019	BAL	MLB	33	31	80	-0.3	.208	0.1		0.0
2020	BAL	MLB	34	251	86	3.3	.284	-0.2	RF -6, 1B 0	-0.2

Mark Trumbo, continued

Batted Ball Distribution

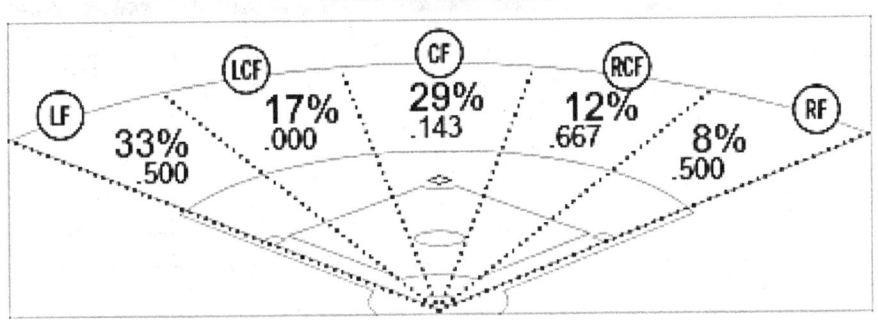

| Strike Zone vs LHP | Strike Zone vs RHP |

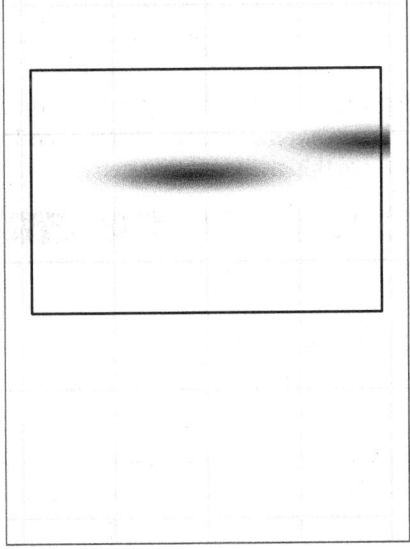

Baltimore Orioles 2020

Richard Ureña MI
Born: 02/26/96 Age: 24 Bats: B Throws: R
Height: 6'0" Weight: 195 Origin: International Free Agent, 2012

YEAR	TEAM	LVL	AGE	PA	R	2B	3B	HR	RBI	BB	K	SB	CS	AVG/OBP/SLG
2017	NHP	AA	21	551	44	36	3	5	60	30	100	0	1	.247/.286/.359
2017	TOR	MLB	21	75	6	4	0	1	4	6	28	1	0	.206/.270/.309
2018	DUN	A+	22	29	2	0	0	0	2	1	6	0	0	.148/.172/.148
2018	BUF	AAA	22	268	28	11	3	5	29	12	48	2	3	.216/.250/.344
2018	TOR	MLB	22	108	10	4	0	1	6	7	32	2	1	.293/.340/.364
2019	BUF	AAA	23	403	43	18	4	6	52	23	85	3	2	.274/.314/.393
2019	TOR	MLB	23	80	4	6	0	0	4	2	23	0	0	.243/.273/.324
2020	TOR	MLB	24	251	22	10	1	6	26	11	70	1	1	.230/.268/.363

Comparables: Amed Rosario, Luis Sardiñas, Ketel Marte

Ureña is a genus of plants common in tropical and subtropical regions. By some the plants are considered weeds, though in other areas they are utilized for their fibers and as food. Ureña could hardly be called invasive, but his continued subtle presence on the Blue Jays—he has received between 75 and 108 plate appearances in each of the past three seasons—points to the organization's continued reliance on a player they might weed out were they in a better place. Strong, versatile defender or not (much like the plant), Ureña and his career .597 OPS do not provide the sustenance Toronto needs and it's only a matter of time before this sixth infielder gets excised from their plans for good.

YEAR	TEAM	LVL	AGE	PA	DRC+	VORP	BABIP	BRR	FRAA	WARP
2017	NHP	AA	21	551	74	6.0	.294	-1.9	SS(115): -4.6, 2B(11): 0.2	0.2
2017	TOR	MLB	21	75	60	0.5	.333	1.4	SS(20): -2.0, 2B(1): 0.1	-0.1
2018	DUN	A+	22	29	33	-3.3	.182	0.1	SS(3): 0.0, 2B(3): -0.4	-0.1
2018	BUF	AAA	22	268	57	-4.7	.246	-0.6	SS(43): 1.8, 2B(17): 0.9	0.1
2018	TOR	MLB	22	108	72	0.5	.424	-1.2	SS(20): -1.3, 2B(13): -1.0	-0.3
2019	BUF	AAA	23	403	80	1.2	.336	1.2	SS(56): 4.8, 2B(39): -0.1	1.1
2019	TOR	MLB	23	80	61	-0.7	.353	-0.8	SS(13): -1.1, 2B(9): -0.8	-0.3
2020	TOR	MLB	24	251	63	-4.3	.300	-0.3	SS -1, 2B -1	-0.6

Richard Ureña, continued

Batted Ball Distribution

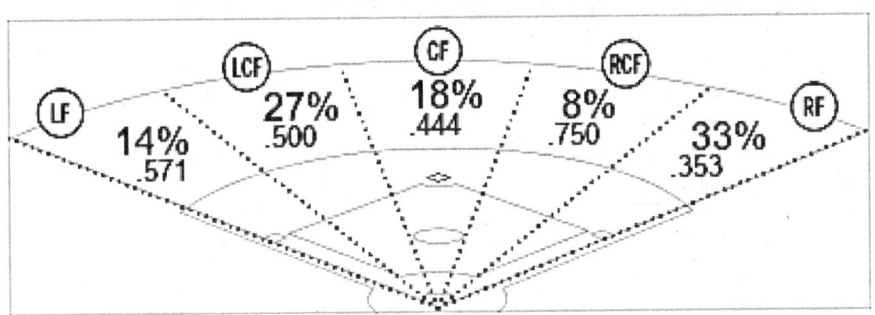

Strike Zone vs LHP   Strike Zone vs RHP

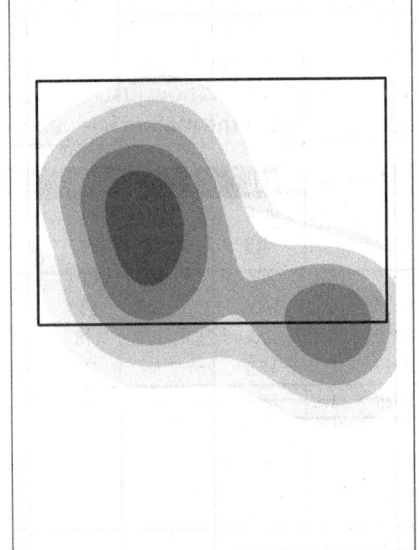

Baltimore Orioles 2020

Pat Valaika INF
Born: 09/09/92   Age: 27   Bats: R   Throws: R
Height: 5'11"   Weight: 208   Origin: Round 9, 2013 Draft (#259 overall)

YEAR	TEAM	LVL	AGE	PA	R	2B	3B	HR	RBI	BB	K	SB	CS	AVG/OBP/SLG
2017	ABQ	AAA	24	50	6	2	1	1	11	4	11	0	0	.267/.327/.422
2017	COL	MLB	24	195	28	11	0	13	40	7	53	0	0	.258/.284/.533
2018	ABQ	AAA	25	147	13	4	1	8	20	7	30	1	1	.216/.252/.432
2018	COL	MLB	25	133	8	5	0	2	5	9	30	0	0	.156/.214/.246
2019	ABQ	AAA	26	383	60	26	1	22	75	27	90	5	1	.320/.364/.589
2019	COL	MLB	26	86	11	5	1	1	4	7	34	0	0	.190/.256/.316
2020	BAL	MLB	27	105	11	4	0	5	14	6	32	1	1	.221/.266/.417

Comparables: Gil McDougald, Cody Asche, Will Middlebrooks

Patty Barrels lived up to his nickname in the PCL, even if Statcast wasn't available to tell us how many of his 22 dingers were verified barrels of the MLBAM variety. That did nothing to help him improve upon his woeful 2018 showing at the major-league level, where he met the bare minimum required to keep that nickname. With a second straight sub-replacement performance, he dropped dangerously close to surrendering the Valaika family WARP title to brother Chris, who is now just 0.3 WARP behind Pat's plummeting mark despite last appearing in the majors five years ago.

YEAR	TEAM	LVL	AGE	PA	DRC+	VORP	BABIP	BRR	FRAA	WARP
2017	ABQ	AAA	24	50	77	1.3	.333	0.5	SS(9): 0.3, 1B(2): 0.0	0.2
2017	COL	MLB	24	195	96	10.8	.291	2.1	SS(22): -0.6, 3B(19): -0.1	0.7
2018	ABQ	AAA	25	147	67	-2.2	.216	-0.6	2B(9): 0.1, SS(9): 0.4	-0.1
2018	COL	MLB	25	133	63	-8.0	.189	0.3	2B(17): -0.6, 1B(15): -0.4	-0.3
2019	ABQ	AAA	26	383	118	24.8	.370	1.0	2B(35): 1.1, SS(18): -1.4	2.3
2019	COL	MLB	26	86	60	-1.5	.318	0.0	2B(13): -0.8, SS(7): 0.1	-0.2
2020	BAL	MLB	27	105	70	-0.1	.276	0.3	2B 0, 3B 0	0.0

Pat Valaika, continued

Batted Ball Distribution

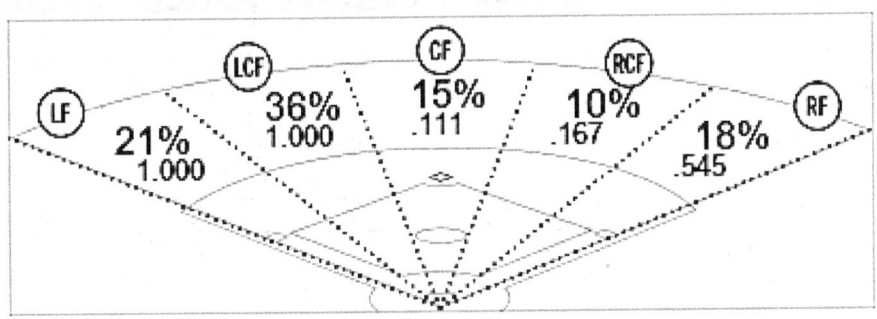

Strike Zone vs LHP   Strike Zone vs RHP

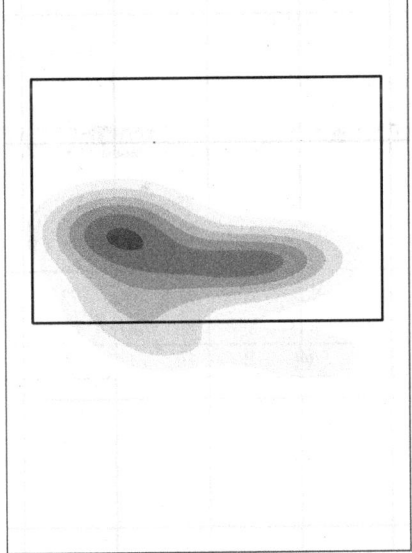

Baltimore Orioles 2020

Stevie Wilkerson OF

Born: 01/11/92 Age: 28 Bats: B Throws: R
Height: 6'1" Weight: 195 Origin: Round 8, 2014 Draft (#241 overall)

YEAR	TEAM	LVL	AGE	PA	R	2B	3B	HR	RBI	BB	K	SB	CS	AVG/OBP/SLG
2017	FRD	A+	25	180	29	10	0	2	15	19	40	2	3	.323/.407/.426
2017	BOW	AA	25	273	34	13	0	6	30	20	53	5	2	.294/.354/.420
2018	NOR	AAA	26	86	13	5	0	4	13	5	15	0	1	.270/.329/.500
2018	BAL	MLB	26	49	2	3	0	0	3	3	16	1	0	.174/.224/.239
2019	NOR	AAA	27	67	13	0	1	2	10	3	9	3	0	.323/.354/.452
2019	BAL	MLB	27	361	41	18	2	10	35	22	108	3	3	.225/.286/.383
2020	BAL	MLB	28	210	20	9	1	5	22	13	60	2	1	.228/.285/.364

Comparables: Danny Klassen, Jonathan Schoop, Tommy Manzella

The pre-2019 edition of Wilkerson played all over the infield dirt and was groomed to be a homegrown utility solution on a team that spent most of the decade overpaying bad ones. The 2019 edition never played center field as a pro but started there a team-high 52 times for the Orioles; had never pitched as a pro but made four appearances off the mound. He even earned the first ever save recorded by a position player on July 25 against the Angels. His manager called him "Dr. Poo Poo." Who said rebuilds aren't fun?

YEAR	TEAM	LVL	AGE	PA	DRC+	VORP	BABIP	BRR	FRAA	WARP
2017	FRD	A+	25	180	143	11.1	.425	1.0	2B(26): -0.5, 3B(8): 0.6	1.5
2017	BOW	AA	25	273	110	11.5	.351	-0.5	3B(37): -0.6, 2B(28): 0.8	1.2
2018	NOR	AAA	26	86	122	6.0	.276	0.2	2B(10): 2.7, 3B(6): 0.3	0.8
2018	BAL	MLB	26	49	64	-3.7	.267	-0.6	2B(9): 0.9, 3B(6): 0.2	0.0
2019	NOR	AAA	27	67	92	2.1	.353	0.2	2B(10): 0.6, 3B(3): 0.1	0.2
2019	BAL	MLB	27	361	66	-3.5	.300	-1.9	CF(72): -8.3, LF(29): -3.5	-1.6
2020	BAL	MLB	28	210	67	-1.6	.302	-0.6	2B 3, SS -1	0.1

Stevie Wilkerson, continued

Batted Ball Distribution

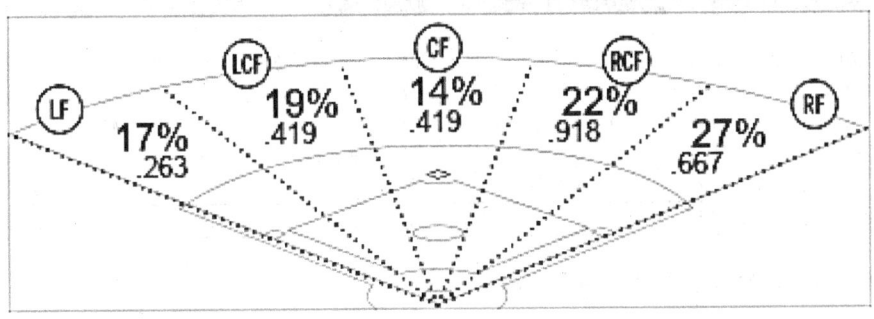

Strike Zone vs LHP   **Strike Zone vs RHP**

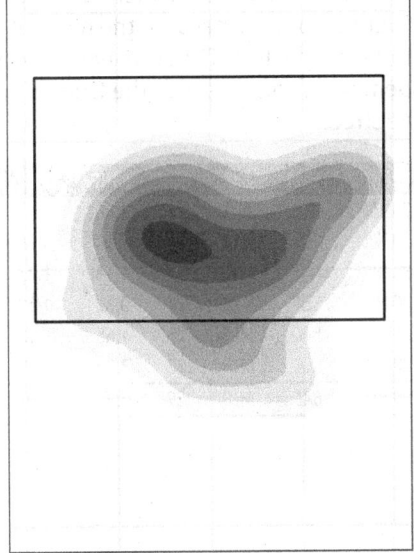

Shawn Armstrong RHP

Born: 09/11/90 Age: 29 Bats: R Throws: R
Height: 6'2" Weight: 225 Origin: Round 18, 2011 Draft (#548 overall)

YEAR	TEAM	LVL	AGE	W	L	SV	G	GS	IP	H	HR	BB/9	K/9	K	GB%	BABIP
2017	COH	AAA	26	1	1	10	28	0	29^1	27	3	3.4	11.0	36	48%	.324
2017	CLE	MLB	26	1	0	0	21	0	24^2	23	5	3.6	7.3	20	40%	.250
2018	TAC	AAA	27	2	5	15	49	0	56	38	3	4.2	13.2	82	35%	.294
2018	SEA	MLB	27	0	1	1	14	0	14^2	9	1	1.8	9.2	15	44%	.229
2019	BAL	MLB	28	1	0	4	51	0	54^1	58	7	4.3	9.9	60	31%	.336
2019	SEA	MLB	28	0	1	0	4	0	3^2	8	1	7.4	7.4	3	25%	.467
2020	BAL	MLB	29	2	2	0	48	0	51	48	9	3.9	8.9	50	34%	.286

Comparables: Santiago Casilla, Sam Tuivailala, J.J. Hoover

Mike Wright was an East Carolina product with a big fastball who got a million chances with the Orioles and was finally cut loose in April. Armstrong, his college teammate and close friend, was cut by the Mariners that same weekend. They switched places, switched numbers (43) and Armstrong continued on with Wright's work. He became the new Mike Wright, right down to the ERA that started with a five. The stuff, however, is better than Wright's and Armstrong spent most of the year as the Orioles' top set-up man before struggling down the stretch.

YEAR	TEAM	LVL	AGE	WHIP	ERA	DRA	WARP	MPH	FB%	WHF	CSP
2017	COH	AAA	26	1.30	3.07	3.82	0.5				
2017	CLE	MLB	26	1.34	4.38	5.02	0.0	95.1	63.5	11.6	50.9
2018	TAC	AAA	27	1.14	1.77	2.45	1.7				
2018	SEA	MLB	27	0.82	1.23	4.40	0.1	95.7	39.2	12.7	52.1
2019	BAL	MLB	28	1.55	5.13	5.43	0.0	95.4	58.8	12.7	50.4
2019	SEA	MLB	28	3.00	14.73	7.26	-0.1	94.5	57.8	16.7	54.5
2020	BAL	MLB	29	1.38	4.92	4.54	0.4	94.7	57.5	12.8	51.2

Shawn Armstrong, continued

Pitch Shape vs LHH

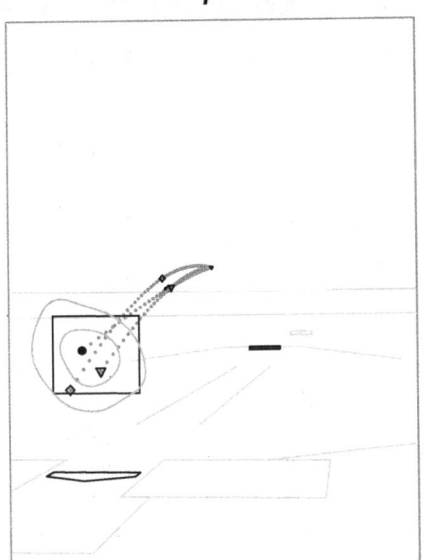

Pitch Shape vs RHH

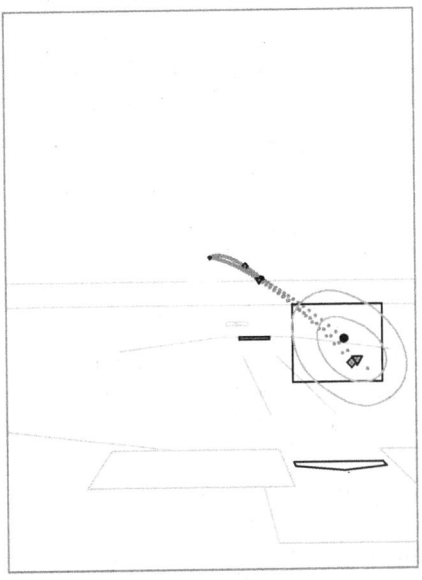

Type	Frequency	Velocity	H Movement	V Movement
● Fastball	58.7%	93.9 [104]	-4.8 [109]	-12.8 [108]
☐ Sinker				
+ Cutter				
▲ Changeup				
✕ Splitter				
▽ Slider	28.7%	90.3 [125]	4.6 [98]	-21.8 [133]
◇ Curveball	12.5%	83.3 [116]	11.6 [117]	-37.4 [122]
⊕ Slow Curveball				
✱ Knuckleball				
▼ Screwball				

Baltimore Orioles 2020

Ty Blach LHP

Born: 10/20/90 Age: 29 Bats: R Throws: L
Height: 6'1" Weight: 213 Origin: Round 5, 2012 Draft (#178 overall)

YEAR	TEAM	LVL	AGE	W	L	SV	G	GS	IP	H	HR	BB/9	K/9	K	GB%	BABIP
2017	SFN	MLB	26	8	12	0	34	24	163^2	179	17	2.4	4.0	73	48%	.290
2018	SFN	MLB	27	6	7	0	47	13	118^2	133	8	3.1	5.7	75	55%	.323
2019	SAC	AAA	28	3	4	0	17	15	91	121	14	2.5	6.4	65	50%	.346
2019	BAL	MLB	28	1	3	0	5	5	20^2	32	6	5.7	7.4	17	34%	.388
2019	SFN	MLB	28	0	0	0	2	0	6^1	14	2	5.7	4.3	3	34%	.444
2020	BAL	MLB	29	2	2	0	33	0	35	42	5	2.9	5.8	23	46%	.316

Comparables: Tom Urbani, T.J. McFarland, Ryan Weber

There are plenty of ways for pitchers to be successful; few, if any, involve a 6.3 percent swinging strike rate. Blach has spent over three years as a swingman/fifth starter type after his debut in September 2016. Since then, no pitcher who has thrown as many innings as Blach has posted a lower strikeout rate (4.9 per nine and 12.7 percent of plate appearances). His innate inability to miss bats didn't stop the Orioles from taking a shot on him in 2019 because he was a living, breathing pitcher with serviceable Triple-A stats. But his hard and soft contact rates are going in the wrong directions, and the way opposing hitters square him up, those lasers are hard to, ahem, block.

YEAR	TEAM	LVL	AGE	WHIP	ERA	DRA	WARP	MPH	FB%	WHF	CSP
2017	SFN	MLB	26	1.36	4.78	4.75	1.5	91.9	60.1	7	50.5
2018	SFN	MLB	27	1.47	4.25	4.79	0.5	92.0	57.6	7.9	50.3
2019	SAC	AAA	28	1.60	5.93	5.69	0.9				
2019	BAL	MLB	28	2.18	11.32	10.61	-1.1	91.9	55.5	8.1	49.1
2019	SFN	MLB	28	2.84	14.21	9.42	-0.3	92.5	60.6	3.9	47.4
2020	BAL	MLB	29	1.51	5.61	5.31	0.0	91.3	58.5	7.4	49.7

Ty Blach, continued

Pitch Shape vs LHH

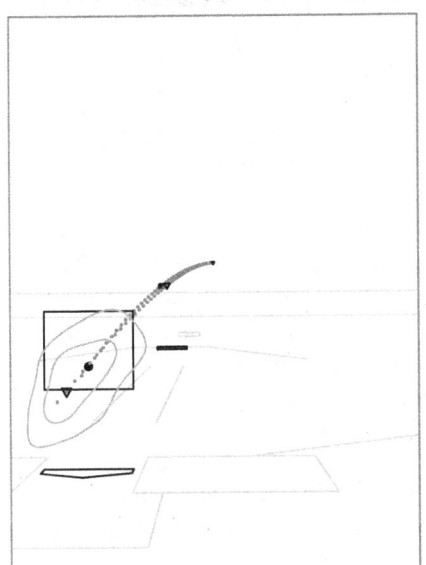

Pitch Shape vs RHH

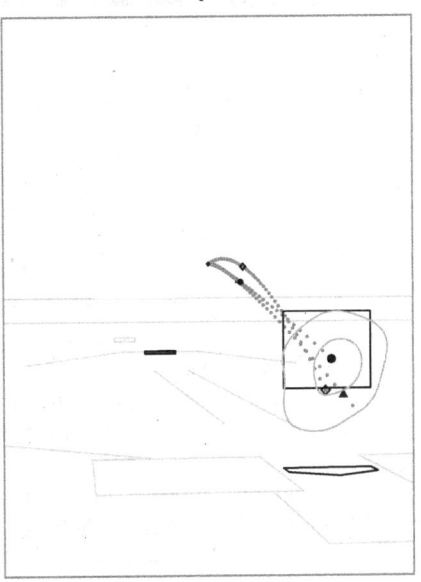

Type	Frequency	Velocity	H Movement	V Movement
● Fastball	56.7%	90.4 [94]	13.7 [70]	-20.9 [87]
□ Sinker				
+ Cutter				
▲ Changeup	26.0%	79.9 [81]	15.2 [81]	-33.4 [82]
✕ Splitter				
▽ Slider	8.7%	84.2 [99]	-0.6 [82]	-29.7 [110]
◇ Curveball	8.7%	77.1 [95]	-6.1 [94]	-50.7 [93]
⊕ Slow Curveball				
✻ Knuckleball				
▼ Screwball				

Richard Bleier LHP

Born: 04/16/87 Age: 33 Bats: L Throws: L
Height: 6'3" Weight: 215 Origin: Round 6, 2008 Draft (#183 overall)

YEAR	TEAM	LVL	AGE	W	L	SV	G	GS	IP	H	HR	BB/9	K/9	K	GB%	BABIP
2017	NOR	AAA	30	0	0	1	8	0	14^2	9	0	0.0	9.2	15	70%	.243
2017	BAL	MLB	30	2	1	0	57	0	63^1	62	6	1.8	3.7	26	69%	.259
2018	BAL	MLB	31	3	0	0	31	0	32^2	36	0	1.1	4.1	15	58%	.319
2019	BAL	MLB	32	3	0	4	53	1	55^1	65	6	1.3	4.9	30	60%	.321
2020	BAL	MLB	33	3	3	3	54	0	57	64	8	1.8	5.2	33	60%	.297

Comparables: Chris Rusin, Steven Wright, Blaine Hardy

Chris Davis got all the attention for starting the Orioles' major dugout altercation of the season with manager Brandon Hyde, but Bleier's a few weeks later was far more effective. All Davis got for his dust-up was a cut in his playing time. Bleier let third base coach José David Flóres know he didn't appreciate the Orioles' infield positioning on a single through the right side that had double-play potential, but instead contributed to a three-run inning on Aug. 28 against Washington. The consequence? Bleier got a straight-up defense the last month of the season, and allowed three runs and just eight baserunners in 11 appearances the rest of the way. The batted-ball misfortune of the preceding five months is reflected above.

YEAR	TEAM	LVL	AGE	WHIP	ERA	DRA	WARP	MPH	FB%	WHF	CSP
2017	NOR	AAA	30	0.61	0.61	2.17	0.5				
2017	BAL	MLB	30	1.18	1.99	5.01	0.1	91.2	62.8	10	52.7
2018	BAL	MLB	31	1.22	1.93	5.09	-0.1	90.2	61.2	10	53.6
2019	BAL	MLB	32	1.32	5.37	5.22	0.1	90.9	64.7	8.8	53.1
2020	BAL	MLB	33	1.32	4.82	4.59	0.4	89.8	62.6	9.4	52.5

Richard Bleier, continued

Pitch Shape vs LHH

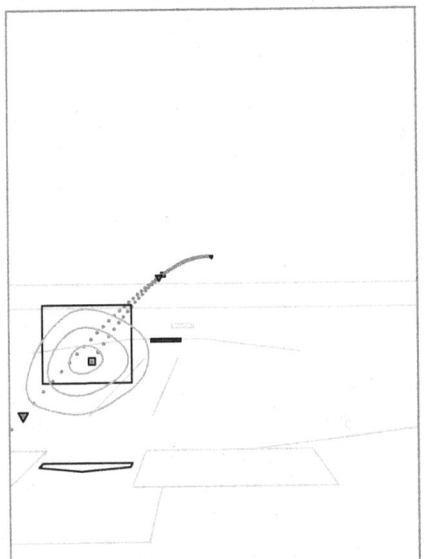

Pitch Shape vs RHH

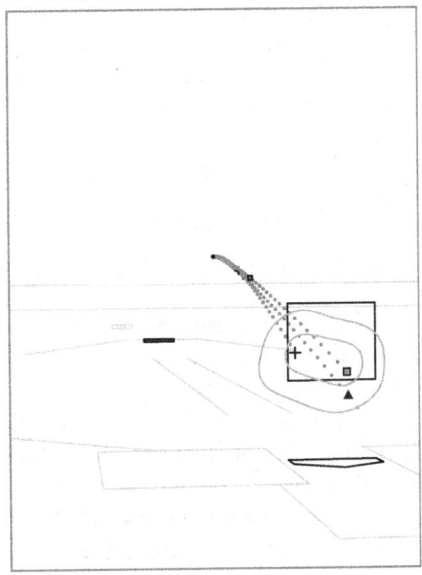

Type	Frequency	Velocity	H Movement	V Movement
● Fastball				
☐ Sinker	62.2%	89.5 [84]	12.3 [102]	-27.1 [76]
+ Cutter	24.1%	87.9 [95]	0.8 [84]	-26.2 [92]
▲ Changeup	4.9%	81.8 [88]	13.4 [90]	-32.4 [85]
✕ Splitter				
▽ Slider	6.3%	80 [81]	-2.5 [90]	-40.1 [80]
◇ Curveball				
✦ Slow Curveball				
✱ Knuckleball				
▼ Screwball				

Orioles Player Analysis - 65

Aaron Brooks   RHP

Born: 04/27/90   Age: 30   Bats: R   Throws: R
Height: 6'4"   Weight: 230   Origin: Round 9, 2011 Draft (#276 overall)

YEAR	TEAM	LVL	AGE	W	L	SV	G	GS	IP	H	HR	BB/9	K/9	K	GB%	BABIP
2017	IOW	AAA	27	8	9	0	24	24	138	181	27	1.8	6.8	105	50%	.345
2017	CSP	AAA	27	0	1	0	2	2	7^2	11	2	1.2	2.3	2	50%	.300
2018	CSP	AAA	28	9	4	0	26	15	99^1	100	8	2.5	6.7	74	56%	.307
2018	OAK	MLB	28	0	0	0	3	0	2^2	1	0	6.8	3.4	1	71%	.143
2019	BAL	MLB	29	4	5	0	14	12	59^2	69	9	3.0	5.9	39	47%	.311
2019	OAK	MLB	29	2	3	0	15	6	50^1	49	12	2.5	7.7	43	41%	.261
2020	BAL	MLB	30	2	2	0	33	0	35	37	6	2.6	6.5	25	47%	.293

Comparables: Tyler Wilson, Zach Neal, Justin Haley

Brooks was an opener, a starter, a bulk reliever and a short reliever in a unique year spent between Oakland and Baltimore, but none of those roles really address what the otherwise-useful sinkerballer truly struggled with: getting outs right as he entered a game. Brooks allowed a .310 average with a .918 OPS in his first 25 pitches of an outing, and after he settled in, it was a .248 average with a .780 OPS. He was far better coming out of the bullpen, whether the expectation was to pitch one inning or seven. Yet, the KIA Tigers are likely to use him as one of their top starters as Brooks inked a deal to give the KBO a whirl in 2020.

YEAR	TEAM	LVL	AGE	WHIP	ERA	DRA	WARP	MPH	FB%	WHF	CSP
2017	IOW	AAA	27	1.51	6.20	6.16	-0.7				
2017	CSP	AAA	27	1.57	4.70	6.04	0.0				
2018	CSP	AAA	28	1.29	3.35	2.96	2.8				
2018	OAK	MLB	28	1.12	0.00	4.72	0.0	94.4	45.2	0	43.4
2019	BAL	MLB	29	1.49	6.18	5.87	-0.1	93.9	50.3	8.5	47.9
2019	OAK	MLB	29	1.25	5.01	6.35	-0.4	94.6	58.4	9.5	47.6
2020	BAL	MLB	30	1.35	4.92	4.82	0.1	93.5	53.6	8.8	45.7

Aaron Brooks, continued

Pitch Shape vs LHH

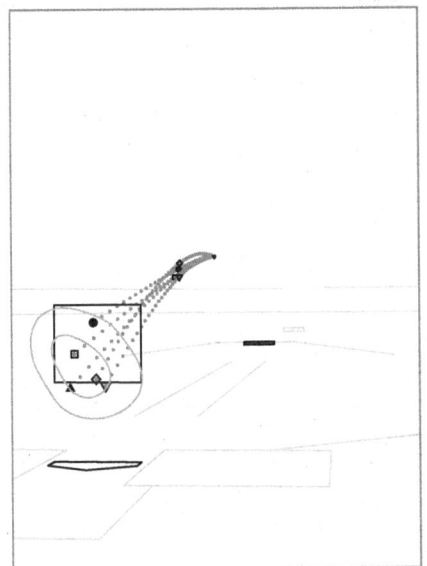

Pitch Shape vs RHH

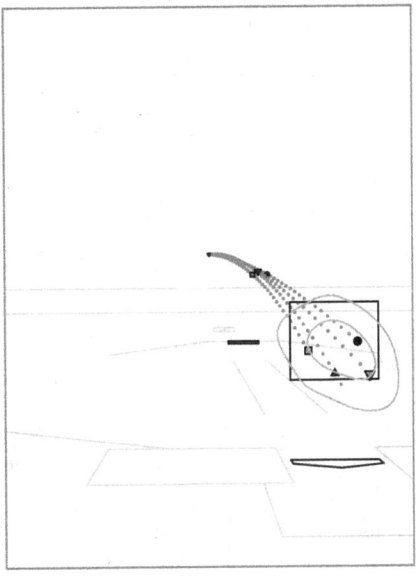

Type	Frequency	Velocity	H Movement	V Movement
● Fastball	22.5%	92.5 [100]	-10.1 [86]	-15.5 [101]
□ Sinker	31.4%	92.2 [98]	-14.5 [88]	-20.2 [100]
+ Cutter				
▲ Changeup	20.4%	85.1 [99]	-12.4 [94]	-33.3 [83]
✕ Splitter				
▽ Slider	22.2%	86 [107]	1.7 [86]	-31.2 [105]
◇ Curveball	3.5%	79.2 [102]	3.2 [83]	-43.2 [109]
⊕ Slow Curveball				
✱ Knuckleball				
▼ Screwball				

Orioles Player Analysis - 67

Baltimore Orioles 2020

Miguel Castro RHP
Born: 12/24/94 Age: 25 Bats: R Throws: R
Height: 6'7" Weight: 205 Origin: International Free Agent, 2012

YEAR	TEAM	LVL	AGE	W	L	SV	G	GS	IP	H	HR	BB/9	K/9	K	GB%	BABIP
2017	BOW	AA	22	3	0	0	6	0	24^1	23	1	2.2	4.1	11	49%	.275
2017	BAL	MLB	22	3	3	0	39	1	66^1	53	8	3.8	5.2	38	50%	.227
2018	BAL	MLB	23	2	7	0	63	1	86^1	75	9	5.2	5.9	57	49%	.259
2019	BAL	MLB	24	1	3	2	65	0	73^1	63	10	5.0	8.7	71	48%	.269
2020	BAL	MLB	25	3	3	0	60	0	64	60	9	4.5	8.3	59	48%	.288

Comparables: Gary Ross, Brad Keller, Aaron Sanchez

Hard as it is to consistently throw a fastball in the upper 90s and hit triple-digits in a big-league game—Castro was one of 37 pitchers to do in 2019—it is apparently much harder to be convinced not to throw it as often. Castro's two-seamer was touched up to the tune of a .346 average and a .583 slugging percentage in 2019, accounting for 70 percent of his homers allowed and 75 percent of his doubles. Meanwhile, his slider and change languished with 37.5 and 39.8 percent whiff rates, respectively. He doesn't command either terribly consistently—mechanics are hard when you're 6-foot-7—and fastball counts typically result in loud sounds when fastballs are thrown. It seems like there's a usage issue that can help Castro become the reliever his stuff has always teased.

YEAR	TEAM	LVL	AGE	WHIP	ERA	DRA	WARP	MPH	FB%	WHF	CSP
2017	BOW	AA	22	1.19	4.44	4.38	0.1				
2017	BAL	MLB	22	1.22	3.53	5.51	-0.2	98.7	61.4	10.5	45.9
2018	BAL	MLB	23	1.45	3.96	6.49	-1.5	98.7	58.1	10.4	47.8
2019	BAL	MLB	24	1.42	4.66	4.02	1.1	99.5	49.1	12.2	45.7
2020	BAL	MLB	25	1.44	4.69	4.32	0.6	98.7	56.4	11.4	47.6

Miguel Castro, continued

Pitch Shape vs LHH

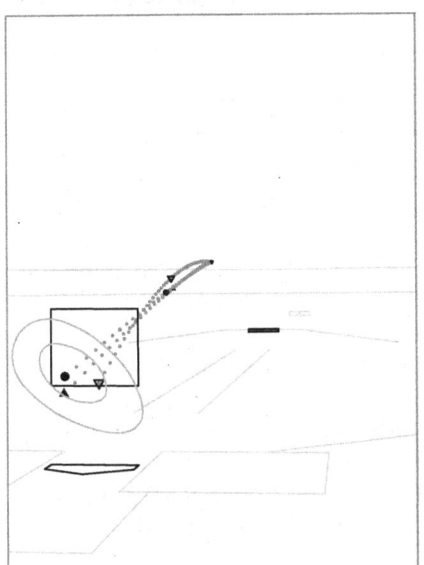

Pitch Shape vs RHH

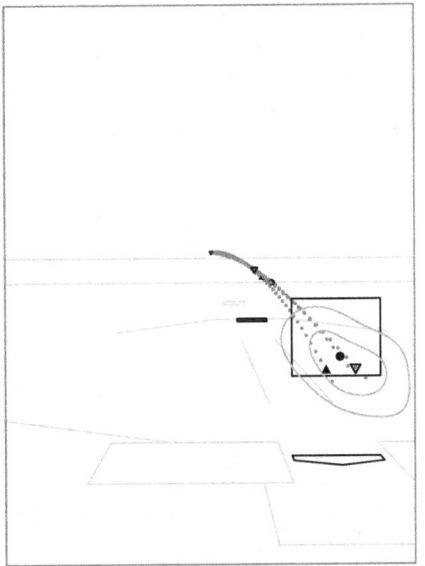

Type	Frequency	Velocity	H Movement	V Movement
● Fastball	49.1%	97.9 [116]	-15.1 [63]	-18.6 [93]
☐ Sinker				
+ Cutter				
▲ Changeup	20.0%	91.1 [121]	-16.3 [76]	-25.7 [105]
✕ Splitter				
▽ Slider	30.9%	86.6 [109]	6.8 [108]	-33 [100]
◇ Curveball				
⊕ Slow Curveball				
✻ Knuckleball				
▼ Screwball				

Alex Cobb RHP

Born: 10/07/87 Age: 32 Bats: R Throws: R
Height: 6'3" Weight: 205 Origin: Round 4, 2006 Draft (#109 overall)

YEAR	TEAM	LVL	AGE	W	L	SV	G	GS	IP	H	HR	BB/9	K/9	K	GB%	BABIP
2017	TBA	MLB	29	12	10	0	29	29	179^1	175	22	2.2	6.4	128	49%	.282
2018	BAL	MLB	30	5	15	0	28	28	152^1	172	24	2.5	6.0	102	51%	.303
2019	BAL	MLB	31	0	2	0	3	3	12^1	21	9	1.5	5.8	8	48%	.293
2020	BAL	MLB	32	8	10	0	26	26	143	176	26	3.0	6.4	102	51%	.324

Comparables: Erik Hanson, John Lackey, Jered Weaver

The former Ray didn't get a spring training after signing his four-year, $57 million contract a week before the 2018 season, instead using the first two months of the season to find his form. He wasn't going to let that happen in 2019, and had command and feel for his vaunted split-change (FKA "The Thing"). He was three good months away from getting out of Baltimore; who wouldn't want a motivated veteran starter whose deferred money was another team's problem? But alas, a groin injury became a back injury, which was traced to a femoroacetabular impingement in his right hip. Just Google it. That was corrected by surgery, so provided his split-change comes back after a long layoff—which didn't happen after his 2015 Tommy John surgery—literally all of that will be the script again.

YEAR	TEAM	LVL	AGE	WHIP	ERA	DRA	WARP	MPH	FB%	WHF	CSP
2017	TBA	MLB	29	1.22	3.66	4.07	3.0	93.5	51.5	7.5	47
2018	BAL	MLB	30	1.41	4.90	5.50	-0.3	93.6	51.5	8	47.6
2019	BAL	MLB	31	1.86	10.95	8.27	-0.3	94.0	47.8	11.4	43.4
2020	BAL	MLB	32	1.57	6.37	5.73	-0.2	92.6	50.8	7.9	45.3

Alex Cobb, continued

Pitch Shape vs LHH

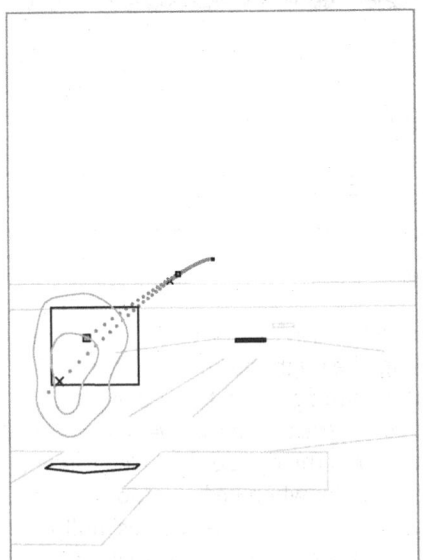

Pitch Shape vs RHH

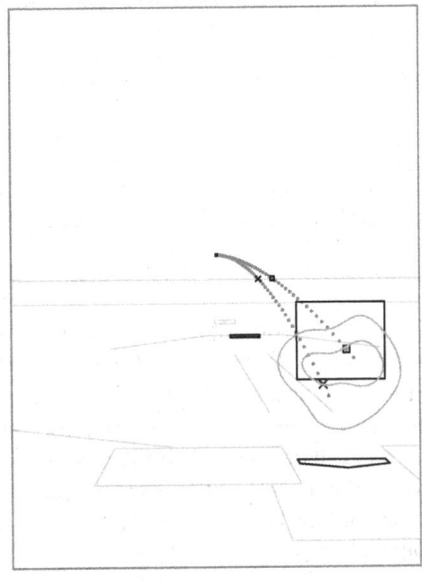

Type	Frequency	Velocity	H Movement	V Movement
● Fastball	3.1%	93 [102]	-10.5 [84]	-12.7 [108]
☐ Sinker	44.7%	92.9 [101]	-12.9 [98]	-17.7 [109]
+ Cutter				
▲ Changeup				
✕ Splitter	35.1%	87.1 [109]	-12 [85]	-28.3 [103]
▽ Slider				
◇ Curveball	17.1%	83.1 [115]	2.5 [80]	-46.7 [102]
⊕ Slow Curveball				
✳ Knuckleball				
▼ Screwball				

Baltimore Orioles 2020

Paul Fry   LHP

Born: 07/26/92   Age: 27   Bats: L   Throws: L
Height: 6'0"   Weight: 190   Origin: Round 17, 2013 Draft (#507 overall)

YEAR	TEAM	LVL	AGE	W	L	SV	G	GS	IP	H	HR	BB/9	K/9	K	GB%	BABIP
2017	BOW	AA	24	0	0	1	7	0	12	7	0	3.8	13.5	18	54%	.292
2017	NOR	AAA	24	3	2	0	25	3	46¹	47	6	5.1	10.3	53	49%	.333
2018	BOW	AA	25	3	0	2	15	0	19	10	2	5.2	13.3	28	68%	.229
2018	NOR	AAA	25	0	1	0	13	1	23¹	22	2	1.5	11.2	29	53%	.345
2018	BAL	MLB	25	1	2	2	35	0	37²	33	1	3.6	8.6	36	58%	.311
2019	BAL	MLB	26	1	9	3	66	0	57¹	54	7	4.6	8.6	55	59%	.297
2020	BAL	MLB	27	2	2	3	42	0	44	42	7	3.6	8.2	41	55%	.284

Comparables: Steven Okert, Eury De La Rosa, Tyler Johnson

The looming three-batter minimum for relievers is, in theory, meant to shake left-handers like Fry out of the majors; though he might be an exception to that rule. The Orioles spent most of the year using him against left-handed hitters, and especially in the second half they ended up greasing him. Five homers in 56 batters will do that. But he struck out a quarter of the righties he faced this year, so maybe there's a little extra mustard on his slider when he backdoors it. Maybe lefties know to avoid that sauce at all costs. Maybe the Orioles' bullpen will be better equipped to put the likes of Fry in better position in 2020 as, eventually, their focus will be on competing as opposed to just running out the clock. Maybe their own data still needs to catch up to this observation. It stands to reason, however, that a lefty reliever who can get righties out will be worth his weight in salt.

YEAR	TEAM	LVL	AGE	WHIP	ERA	DRA	WARP	MPH	FB%	WHF	CSP
2017	BOW	AA	24	1.00	0.75	2.17	0.4				
2017	NOR	AAA	24	1.58	4.66	5.56	-0.1				
2018	BOW	AA	25	1.11	2.84	1.87	0.7				
2018	NOR	AAA	25	1.11	3.47	3.97	0.3				
2018	BAL	MLB	25	1.27	3.35	4.17	0.3	93.3	56.5	10.8	44.6
2019	BAL	MLB	26	1.45	5.34	4.75	0.4	92.8	52.3	10.9	47.1
2020	BAL	MLB	27	1.34	4.57	4.27	0.4	92.5	54.3	11	46.5

Paul Fry, continued

Pitch Shape vs LHH

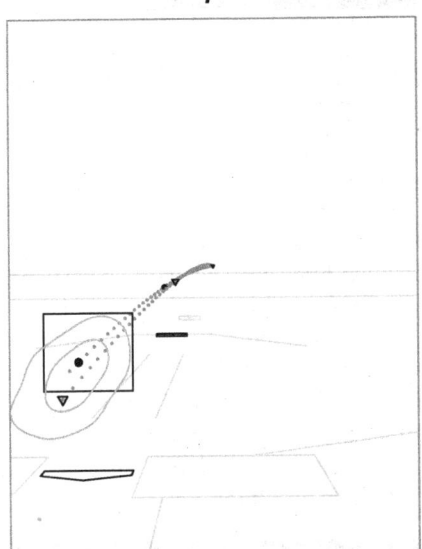

Pitch Shape vs RHH

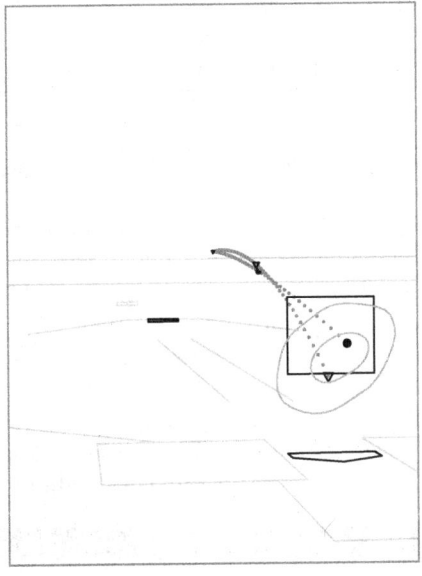

Type	Frequency	Velocity	H Movement	V Movement
● Fastball	52.3%	91.2 [96]	1.9 [122]	-19.3 [91]
☐ Sinker				
+ Cutter				
▲ Changeup				
✕ Splitter				
▽ Slider	46.2%	84.3 [100]	-13.3 [135]	-38.5 [84]
◇ Curveball				
⊕ Slow Curveball				
✳ Knuckleball				
▼ Screwball				

Mychal Givens   RHP

Born: 05/13/90   Age: 30   Bats: R   Throws: R
Height: 6'0"   Weight: 210   Origin: Round 2, 2009 Draft (#54 overall)

YEAR	TEAM	LVL	AGE	W	L	SV	G	GS	IP	H	HR	BB/9	K/9	K	GB%	BABIP
2017	BAL	MLB	27	8	1	0	69	0	78^2	57	10	2.9	10.1	88	43%	.251
2018	BAL	MLB	28	0	7	9	69	0	76^2	61	4	3.5	9.3	79	38%	.284
2019	BAL	MLB	29	2	6	11	58	0	63	49	13	3.7	12.3	86	39%	.271
2020	BAL	MLB	30	3	3	14	54	0	57	47	8	3.6	11.4	73	40%	.293

Comparables: Vinnie Pestano, Arodys Vizcaíno, Tommy Kahnle

Fifty pitchers had at least 25 appearances in save situations in 2019. Only two—Colin Poche and Edwin Díaz—had a higher ERA than Givens' 5.90 in such situations, and two—Josh Hader and Emilio Pagán—allowed more than his eight home runs in them. Simply put, Givens has not been one when it comes to locking down saves. He had a 1.67 ERA before the ninth inning, and a 6.75 ERA in and after it. He's murder on righties, and lefties come calling with the receipts. It's an electric arsenal that will probably make an All-Star team the second he leaves Baltimore and gets to set-up somewhere else, but it's hard to showcase that when he has to pitch in situations he's shown aren't for him.

YEAR	TEAM	LVL	AGE	WHIP	ERA	DRA	WARP	MPH	FB%	WHF	CSP
2017	BAL	MLB	27	1.04	2.75	3.69	1.3	98.0	72.2	13.1	50.3
2018	BAL	MLB	28	1.19	3.99	4.84	0.1	97.8	76.8	12.5	53.1
2019	BAL	MLB	29	1.19	4.57	3.08	1.6	98.0	70.3	17.1	50.4
2020	BAL	MLB	30	1.24	3.89	3.69	0.9	97.1	72.9	14.4	51.1

Mychal Givens, continued

Pitch Shape vs LHH

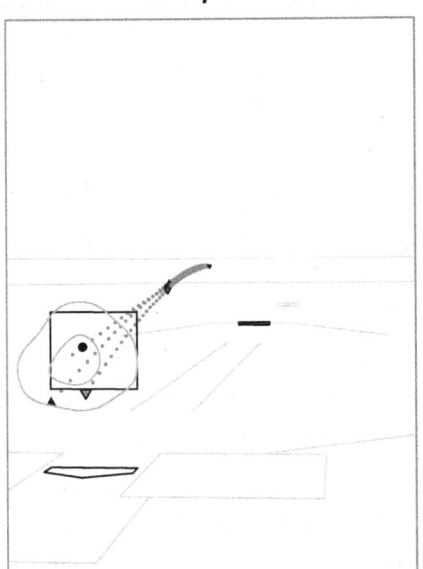

Pitch Shape vs RHH

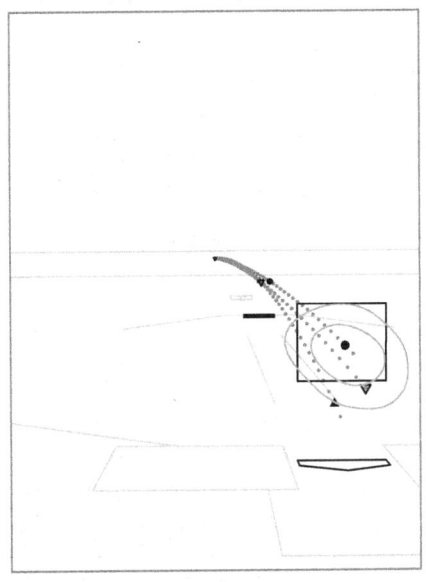

Type	Frequency	Velocity	H Movement	V Movement
● Fastball	70.3%	95.7 [110]	-8.7 [92]	-15.8 [100]
☐ Sinker				
+ Cutter				
▲ Changeup	14.2%	85.1 [99]	-11.2 [100]	-37.1 [72]
✕ Splitter				
▽ Slider	15.5%	87.6 [114]	3.9 [96]	-27.7 [116]
◇ Curveball				
⊕ Slow Curveball				
✳ Knuckleball				
▼ Screwball				

Baltimore Orioles 2020

Hunter Harvey   RHP

Born: 12/09/94 Age: 25 Bats: R Throws: R
Height: 6'3" Weight: 175 Origin: Round 1, 2013 Draft (#22 overall)

YEAR	TEAM	LVL	AGE	W	L	SV	G	GS	IP	H	HR	BB/9	K/9	K	GB%	BABIP
2017	DEL	A	22	0	1	0	3	3	8²	4	0	3.1	14.5	14	31%	.250
2018	BOW	AA	23	1	2	0	9	9	32¹	36	3	2.5	8.4	30	36%	.351
2019	BOW	AA	24	2	5	1	14	11	59	63	14	3.2	9.3	61	40%	.316
2019	NOR	AAA	24	1	1	0	12	0	16²	13	2	2.7	11.9	22	43%	.275
2019	BAL	MLB	24	1	0	0	7	0	6¹	3	1	5.7	15.6	11	55%	.200
2020	BAL	MLB	25	3	3	10	54	0	57	49	8	3.6	10.1	64	39%	.286

Comparables: Keury Mella, Michael Blazek, Wilfredo Boscan

Harvey's long-awaited major-league debut was a bright moment for the 2019 Orioles, considering he'd been injured for all but fleeting spells from July 2014 to this spring. It was only made sweeter by a mullet/mustache combination straight out of "Road House." But he finally made it in a new relief role where his fastball bumped triple digits, his dad's splitter fell out of the zone and his breaking ball flashed. All his presence did was make the miserable Orioles bullpen instantly different. His first outing was low-leverage; his last was 10 days after the preceding one, and then he was shut down for typical September reasons. In between, he was the high-leverage reliever Brandon Hyde never had. The Orioles' bullpen ERA in that two-week span with Harvey pitching the seventh and eighth was 2.58, third-best in the majors. It was 5.98 outside that span. Maybe the mullet is magic.

YEAR	TEAM	LVL	AGE	WHIP	ERA	DRA	WARP	MPH	FB%	WHF	CSP
2017	DEL	A	22	0.81	2.08	2.21	0.3				
2018	BOW	AA	23	1.39	5.57	5.07	0.1				
2019	BOW	AA	24	1.42	5.19	6.42	-1.1				
2019	NOR	AAA	24	1.08	4.32	2.97	0.5				
2019	BAL	MLB	24	1.11	1.42	3.70	0.1	99.8	69.6	12.6	48.2
2020	BAL	MLB	25	1.26	4.08	3.84	0.8	99.5	71.3	12.9	49.3

Hunter Harvey, continued

Pitch Shape vs LHH

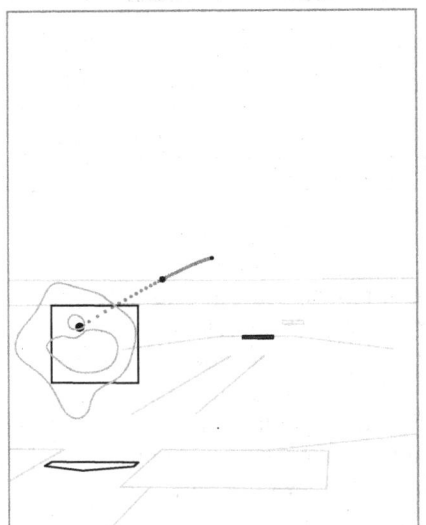

Pitch Shape vs RHH

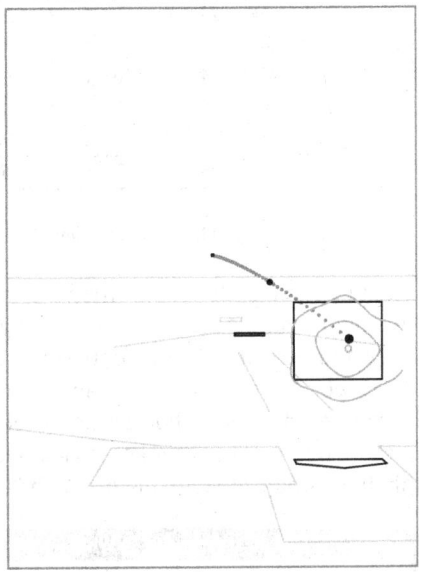

Type	Frequency	Velocity	H Movement	V Movement
● Fastball	69.6%	98.6 [118]	-4.9 [109]	-9.8 [116]
☐ Sinker				
+ Cutter				
▲ Changeup	15.6%	89.9 [117]	-8.1 [114]	-26.1 [104]
✕ Splitter				
▽ Slider				
◇ Curveball	14.8%	83.6 [117]	5.8 [93]	-42.9 [110]
✦ Slow Curveball				
✳ Knuckleball				
▼ Screwball				

Baltimore Orioles 2020

David Hess RHP
Born: 07/10/93 Age: 26 Bats: R Throws: R
Height: 6'2" Weight: 180 Origin: Round 5, 2014 Draft (#151 overall)

YEAR	TEAM	LVL	AGE	W	L	SV	G	GS	IP	H	HR	BB/9	K/9	K	GB%	BABIP
2017	BOW	AA	23	11	9	0	27	26	154^1	137	16	3.1	7.2	123	32%	.269
2018	NOR	AAA	24	3	2	0	9	9	45^2	38	3	3.7	8.7	44	29%	.285
2018	BAL	MLB	24	3	10	0	21	19	103^1	106	22	3.2	6.4	74	35%	.268
2019	NOR	AAA	25	3	2	1	13	4	41^1	41	7	2.6	10.2	47	45%	.312
2019	BAL	MLB	25	1	10	0	23	14	80	94	28	3.4	7.7	68	34%	.278
2020	BAL	MLB	26	2	3	0	35	5	49	57	13	3.5	7.3	39	35%	.304

Comparables: Zeke Spruill, Myles Jaye, Allen Webster

The quiet thing left unsaid when a pitcher is removed late in a no-hitter is that he might not be good enough to ever get that close again. Hess, on the first of April, took one into the seventh on short rest against the Blue Jays but was removed after just 82 pitches and watched from the dugout as Elvis Araujo surrendered a homer two batters later. The strong performance was ultimately just a cruel April Fool's joke, as Hess went on to allow the most home runs of any pitcher in major-league history with 80 innings or fewer.

YEAR	TEAM	LVL	AGE	WHIP	ERA	DRA	WARP	MPH	FB%	WHF	CSP
2017	BOW	AA	23	1.23	3.85	3.60	2.9				
2018	NOR	AAA	24	1.25	3.15	4.40	0.6				
2018	BAL	MLB	24	1.38	4.88	7.38	-2.5	94.6	58.7	9.1	47.9
2019	NOR	AAA	25	1.28	4.57	4.18	0.9				
2019	BAL	MLB	25	1.55	7.09	8.46	-2.4	95.2	59.2	9.5	47.1
2020	BAL	MLB	26	1.57	6.65	5.89	-0.3	94.5	60	9.5	48.3

David Hess, continued

Pitch Shape vs LHH

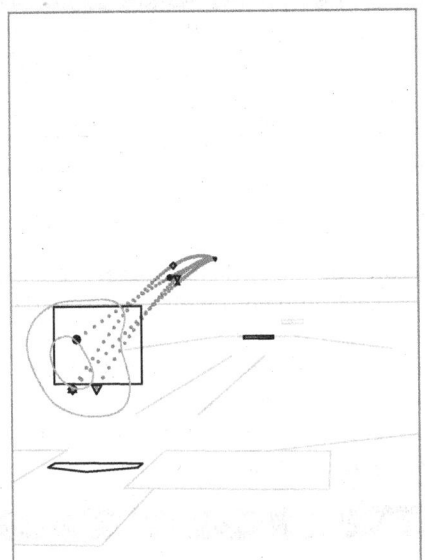

Pitch Shape vs RHH

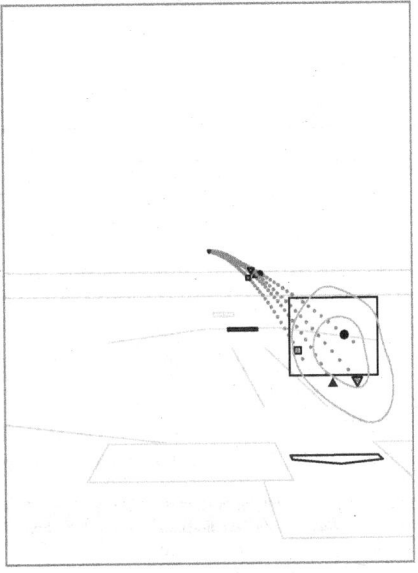

Type	Frequency	Velocity	H Movement	V Movement
● Fastball	53.7%	93.5 [103]	-3 [117]	-13 [108]
□ Sinker	5.5%	92.9 [102]	-11.3 [109]	-15.6 [117]
+ Cutter				
▲ Changeup	11.6%	86.1 [103]	-10.9 [101]	-25.2 [107]
✕ Splitter				
▽ Slider	24.9%	83.8 [98]	4.6 [98]	-31.5 [105]
◇ Curveball	4.3%	77.6 [97]	7 [98]	-44.4 [107]
✦ Slow Curveball				
✱ Knuckleball				
▼ Screwball				

Baltimore Orioles 2020

Branden Kline   RHP
Born: 09/29/91   Age: 28   Bats: R   Throws: R
Height: 6'3"   Weight: 210   Origin: Round 2, 2012 Draft (#65 overall)

YEAR	TEAM	LVL	AGE	W	L	SV	G	GS	IP	H	HR	BB/9	K/9	K	GB%	BABIP
2018	FRD	A+	26	1	0	2	12	0	20²	20	0	1.3	10.0	23	36%	.357
2018	BOW	AA	26	4	4	15	32	0	45	32	3	3.0	9.6	48	45%	.254
2019	NOR	AAA	27	1	1	2	18	0	21	27	4	5.6	11.6	27	43%	.404
2019	BAL	MLB	27	1	4	0	34	0	41	44	9	4.2	7.5	34	40%	.294
2020	BAL	MLB	28	1	1	0	18	0	19	20	3	3.8	8.0	17	41%	.299

Comparables: J.R. Graham, Luis Cessa, Steven Wright

Before the Orioles' young pitchers played catch on the outfield grass every afternoon, they circled up and played hacky sack. And boy oh boy, were they good at hacky sack. Once 7:05 p.m. comes, they all have the raw ingredients to be successful in the majors, if not the consistency. Kline's mid-90s fastball and swing-and-miss slider put him in that category. He, like the rest, could grow into a qualified major-league reliever with experience and refinement. Right now, it's important to note that they are all very, very good at hacky sack.

YEAR	TEAM	LVL	AGE	WHIP	ERA	DRA	WARP	MPH	FB%	WHF	CSP
2018	FRD	A+	26	1.11	1.31	3.65	0.3				
2018	BOW	AA	26	1.04	1.80	2.43	1.3				
2019	NOR	AAA	27	1.90	6.86	6.70	-0.1				
2019	BAL	MLB	27	1.54	5.93	6.10	-0.3	98.8	57.5	11	46.4
2020	BAL	MLB	28	1.45	5.32	4.92	0.1	98.2	57.8	11.1	46.6

Branden Kline, continued

Pitch Shape vs LHH

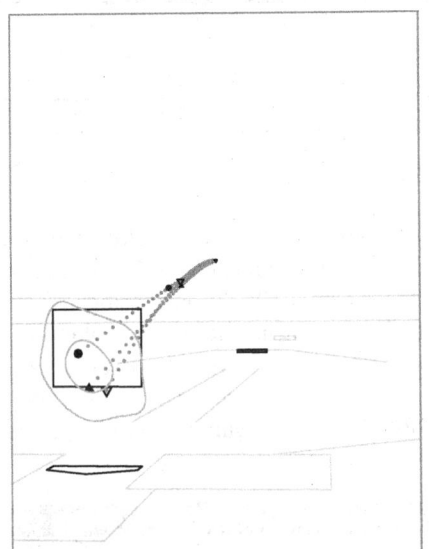

Pitch Shape vs RHH

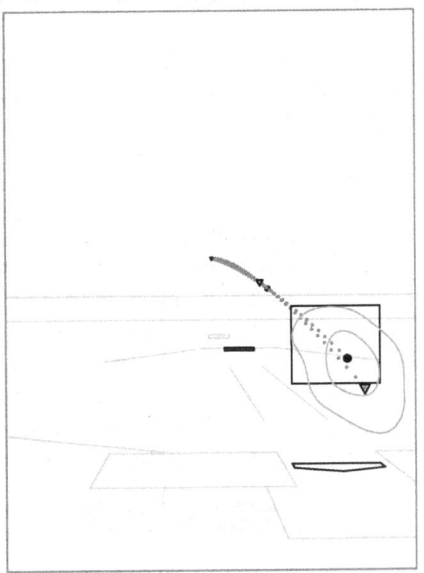

Type	Frequency	Velocity	H Movement	V Movement
● Fastball	57.5%	96.8 [112]	-7.6 [97]	-11.7 [111]
☐ Sinker				
+ Cutter				
▲ Changeup	8.6%	87.9 [110]	-9.8 [106]	-24.7 [108]
✕ Splitter				
▽ Slider	33.9%	87.1 [111]	2.1 [88]	-28.7 [113]
◇ Curveball				
⊕ Slow Curveball				
✱ Knuckleball				
▼ Screwball				

Baltimore Orioles 2020

Wade LeBlanc   LHP

Born: 08/07/84   Age: 35   Bats: L   Throws: L
Height: 6'3"   Weight: 205   Origin: Round 2, 2006 Draft (#61 overall)

YEAR	TEAM	LVL	AGE	W	L	SV	G	GS	IP	H	HR	BB/9	K/9	K	GB%	BABIP
2017	PIT	MLB	32	5	2	1	50	0	68	64	10	2.2	7.1	54	47%	.269
2018	SEA	MLB	33	9	5	0	32	27	162	151	24	2.2	7.2	130	37%	.273
2019	SEA	MLB	34	6	7	0	26	8	121[1]	145	28	2.3	6.8	92	41%	.308
2020	SEA	MLB	35	2	2	0	33	0	35	40	9	2.6	6.9	27	39%	.295

Comparables: Clayton Richard, Jeff Francis, Tommy Milone

The peak of LeBlanc's season came before Opening Day, when he starred in the commercial "Arts and Crafty" alongside fellow left-handers Marco Gonzales and Yusei Kikuchi, a hilarious homage to the team's stockpile of soft-tossing southpaws. His 2018 renaissance was a delightful surprise for the popular veteran, but hitters tend not to be as nice to pitchers of LeBlanc's ilk for extended periods of time. The clock struck 2019, and LeBlanc was a pumpkin once again. The softest-tossing starter not named Jason Vargas was a lot worse than Vargas, which may be all you need to know.

YEAR	TEAM	LVL	AGE	WHIP	ERA	DRA	WARP	MPH	FB%	WHF	CSP
2017	PIT	MLB	32	1.19	4.50	3.77	1.1	88.8	62.9	10.3	46.1
2018	SEA	MLB	33	1.18	3.72	5.07	0.4	88.0	61.1	10.1	47.7
2019	SEA	MLB	34	1.45	5.71	8.04	-3.4	87.6	58.1	10.5	47.9
2020	SEA	MLB	35	1.43	5.80	5.70	-0.2	86.8	59	10.1	46.5

Wade LeBlanc, continued

Pitch Shape vs LHH

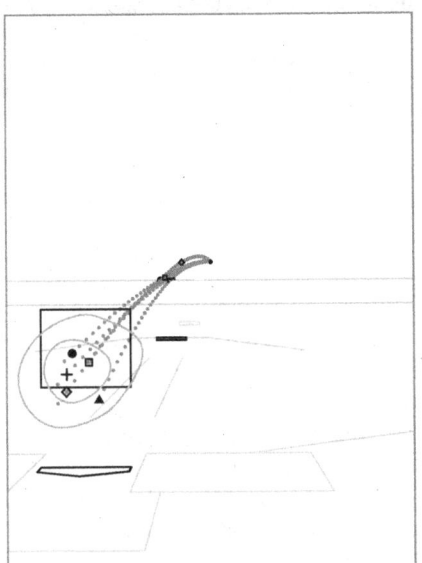

Pitch Shape vs RHH

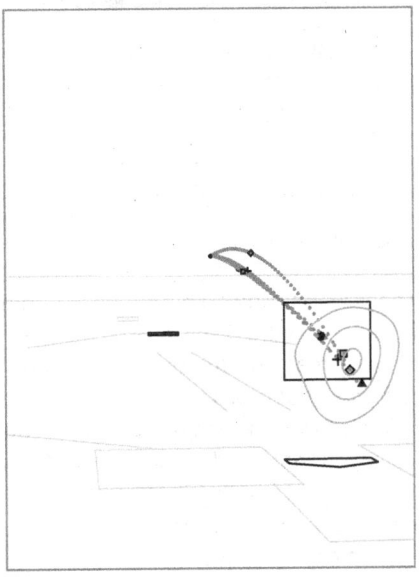

Type	Frequency	Velocity	H Movement	V Movement
● Fastball	4.7%	86.7 [84]	8.7 [92]	-18.9 [92]
☐ Sinker	23.5%	86.5 [68]	13.6 [94]	-23 [91]
+ Cutter	29.9%	84.4 [73]	0.5 [86]	-24.9 [97]
▲ Changeup	30.9%	78.9 [77]	12.9 [92]	-33.4 [82]
✕ Splitter				
▽ Slider				
◇ Curveball	10.5%	72.7 [80]	-10.8 [114]	-53.1 [88]
✦ Slow Curveball				
✱ Knuckleball				
▼ Screwball				

Baltimore Orioles 2020

John Means LHP

Born: 04/24/93 Age: 27 Bats: L Throws: L
Height: 6'3" Weight: 230 Origin: Round 11, 2014 Draft (#331 overall)

YEAR	TEAM	LVL	AGE	W	L	SV	G	GS	IP	H	HR	BB/9	K/9	K	GB%	BABIP
2017	BOW	AA	24	9	9	0	26	24	142^1	158	16	2.3	7.8	124	38%	.322
2018	BOW	AA	25	1	4	0	8	7	46	43	6	2.5	8.0	41	41%	.276
2018	NOR	AAA	25	6	5	0	20	19	111^1	123	9	1.5	7.2	89	35%	.324
2018	BAL	MLB	25	0	0	0	1	0	3^1	6	1	0.0	10.8	4	25%	.455
2019	BAL	MLB	26	12	11	0	31	27	155	138	23	2.2	7.0	121	32%	.256
2020	BAL	MLB	27	10	9	0	28	28	151	141	29	2.3	7.1	120	33%	.259

Comparables: Zach Neal, Tyler Wilson, Joel Payamps

Means was sitting on his couch watching football in September 2018 when he lied and told the Orioles he'd still been throwing and could build back up to possibly make his major-league debut. That was about the only time he was dishonest about his career; he thought he'd be the first spring training cut and bide his time in the minors, but instead, the fruits of a career-changing offseason took hold. He went to a specialized performance center and added three ticks of velocity to his fastball while learning the benefits of locating it up in the zone; then, in spring training, he worked with new pitching guru Chris Holt on developing a changeup that got 13 swinging strikes in his 2019 debut. Means never looked back. He was an All-Star because the changeup punished teams for stacking right-handers against him, and he had enough fastball to trick hitters who looked for the fade. He started throwing a shorter slider that can be a weapon against both sides late in the season.

For an organization that's so committed to player development—more specifically, having those players develop legitimate major-league skills and tools—having someone like Means do what he did as a rookie is a bastion of hope and an example that all this can work. It takes commitment. It takes a willingness to change everything about yourself as a player. It takes a little bit of fortune. And it takes a consistent plan to bring all those things about and put yourself in position to make Giancarlo Stanton whiff so hard it ruined his season. Means went from a fringe minor leaguer to a legitimate major-league starter who could be one of the few players still on the Orioles the next time they're competitive.

YEAR	TEAM	LVL	AGE	WHIP	ERA	DRA	WARP	MPH	FB%	WHF	CSP
2017	BOW	AA	24	1.36	4.11	4.83	0.5				
2018	BOW	AA	25	1.22	4.30	3.84	0.8				
2018	NOR	AAA	25	1.28	3.48	4.97	0.7				
2018	BAL	MLB	25	1.80	13.50	9.83	-0.2	91.7	37.9	12.1	41.7
2019	BAL	MLB	26	1.14	3.60	4.61	1.9	94.0	50.8	10.6	47.1
2020	*BAL*	*MLB*	*27*	*1.19*	*4.25*	*4.10*	*2.5*	*93.5*	*51.1*	*10.8*	*45.2*

Baltimore Orioles 2020

John Means, continued

Pitch Shape vs LHH

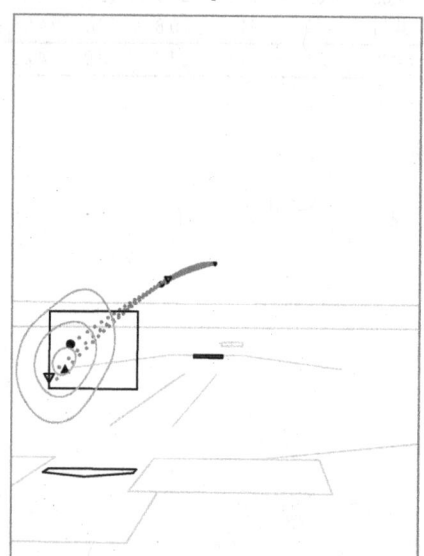

Pitch Shape vs RHH

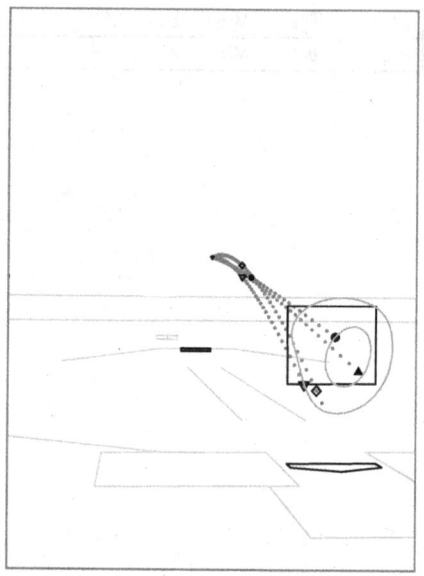

Type	Frequency	Velocity	H Movement	V Movement
● Fastball	50.7%	92.2 [99]	5.3 [107]	-11.7 [111]
☐ Sinker				
+ Cutter				
▲ Changeup	28.9%	81.3 [86]	10.9 [101]	-21.6 [117]
✕ Splitter				
▽ Slider	14.4%	84.1 [99]	-3.8 [95]	-29.1 [112]
◇ Curveball	5.9%	77.1 [95]	-3.1 [82]	-45.2 [105]
⊕ Slow Curveball				
✱ Knuckleball				
▼ Screwball				

Tommy Milone LHP

Born: 02/16/87 Age: 33 Bats: L Throws: L
Height: 6'0" Weight: 215 Origin: Round 10, 2008 Draft (#301 overall)

YEAR	TEAM	LVL	AGE	W	L	SV	G	GS	IP	H	HR	BB/9	K/9	K	GB%	BABIP
2017	BIN	AA	30	1	0	0	4	4	20	26	8	0.9	4.9	11	27%	.273
2017	MIL	MLB	30	1	0	1	6	3	21	29	6	0.9	6.9	16	35%	.333
2017	NYN	MLB	30	0	3	0	11	5	27^1	36	9	4.0	7.2	22	36%	.318
2018	SYR	AAA	31	7	4	0	20	20	109^2	101	11	2.0	9.3	113	36%	.303
2018	WAS	MLB	31	1	1	0	5	4	26^1	37	7	0.3	7.9	23	30%	.349
2019	TAC	AAA	32	4	2	0	9	8	49^1	49	7	2.2	7.8	43	39%	.286
2019	SEA	MLB	32	4	10	0	23	6	111^2	102	24	1.9	7.6	94	38%	.252
2020	SEA	MLB	33	2	2	0	33	0	35	37	9	2.3	7.5	29	37%	.282

Comparables: Wade Miley, Wade LeBlanc, Jason Vargas

Each of Milone's Annual comments in recent years have read with a sense that this could be the last time his name was ever written in one of these hefty books. The notion that his mishmosh of meh pitches from the left side would return the next year to face major-league hitters is increasingly difficult to fathom. And yet, here we are again. 111 2/3 innings, only 108 1/3 more than PECOTA projected a year ago. At this point, Milone has become the baseball version of that friend in college you could always count on to show up to your intramural basketball game. "What's Tommy up to? He's definitely not doing anything and we're not just gonna play with 5 guys. We're gonna need someone to come off the bench." In the context of the 2019 Mariners, someone had to go out there and throw the baseball to the other team's hitters. Here's to another full Milone comment in next year's Annual, somehow, some way.

YEAR	TEAM	LVL	AGE	WHIP	ERA	DRA	WARP	MPH	FB%	WHF	CSP
2017	BIN	AA	30	1.40	4.95	6.48	-0.3				
2017	MIL	MLB	30	1.48	6.43	6.38	-0.2	89.8	65.2	8.3	43.8
2017	NYN	MLB	30	1.76	8.56	5.28	0.1	89.5	65.2	8.9	42.5
2018	SYR	AAA	31	1.14	4.19	4.47	1.3				
2018	WAS	MLB	31	1.44	5.81	4.64	0.2	88.8	58.9	11.7	46.9
2019	TAC	AAA	32	1.24	3.83	3.06	1.7				
2019	SEA	MLB	32	1.12	4.76	5.68	-0.3	88.6	43.7	10.5	45.8
2020	SEA	MLB	33	1.32	5.18	5.27	0.0	87.8	49.5	10.2	44.9

Baltimore Orioles 2020

Tommy Milone, continued

Pitch Shape vs LHH

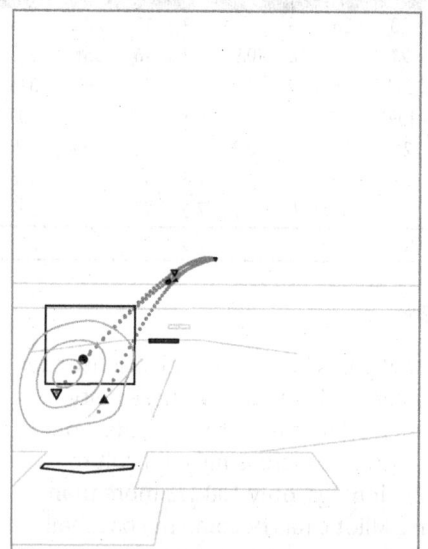

Pitch Shape vs RHH

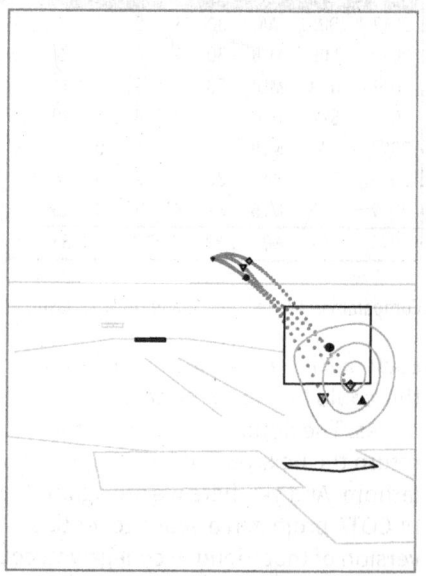

Type	Frequency	Velocity	H Movement	V Movement
● Fastball	43.7%	87.4 [86]	7.4 [98]	-16.2 [99]
☐ Sinker				
+ Cutter				
▲ Changeup	38.1%	79.7 [80]	13.9 [87]	-31.8 [87]
✕ Splitter				
▽ Slider	14.9%	78.1 [74]	-3.6 [94]	-39.6 [81]
◇ Curveball	3.2%	75.9 [91]	-3.5 [84]	-45.6 [104]
⊕ Slow Curveball				
✳ Knuckleball				
▼ Screwball				

Evan Phillips   RHP

Born: 09/11/94   Age: 25   Bats: R   Throws: R
Height: 6'2"   Weight: 215   Origin: Round 17, 2015 Draft (#510 overall)

YEAR	TEAM	LVL	AGE	W	L	SV	G	GS	IP	H	HR	BB/9	K/9	K	GB%	BABIP
2017	MIS	AA	22	1	1	1	15	0	21	22	5	4.7	10.3	24	47%	.321
2017	GWN	AAA	22	2	3	2	25	1	30^1	30	1	6.8	8.6	29	46%	.345
2018	GWN	AAA	23	4	4	8	31	0	40^2	28	1	3.1	13.1	59	51%	.325
2018	NOR	AAA	23	0	2	0	8	0	10^2	6	1	2.5	11.0	13	32%	.208
2018	ATL	MLB	23	0	0	0	4	0	6^1	6	3	5.7	4.3	3	41%	.158
2018	BAL	MLB	23	0	1	0	5	1	5^1	7	2	10.1	8.4	5	39%	.312
2019	NOR	AAA	24	1	2	1	27	0	39^2	35	2	3.9	10.0	44	50%	.324
2019	BAL	MLB	24	0	1	0	25	0	28	32	2	6.4	12.9	40	40%	.411
2020	BAL	MLB	25	1	1	0	24	0	25	25	4	4.3	9.9	28	42%	.310

Comparables: Eduardo Paredes, Andrew Bellatti, Jake Newberry

One of the most frequent shuttle-riders between Triple-A Norfolk and Baltimore, Phillips was called up eight different times, and pitched on seven of those occasions. Here is how he re-introduced himself with his first batter. April 9: walk. May 26: walk. June 7: pop fly, (followed immediately by a walk). June 20: strikeout! But, then an RBI-single July 27: lineout! But, then a home run. August 12: three-run home run. Sept. 7: lineout, then two strikeouts. September was a good month because he attacked the strike zone far more often, and didn't give up a run until the last day of the season. The 2020 roster changes will eliminate the chance for these types to pitch well knowing they don't need to fear being sent down in September, and that's a shame. How will we know which 95-and-a-slider reliever might turn the corner?

YEAR	TEAM	LVL	AGE	WHIP	ERA	DRA	WARP	MPH	FB%	WHF	CSP
2017	MIS	AA	22	1.57	8.14	5.85	-0.3				
2017	GWN	AAA	22	1.75	4.75	5.97	-0.2				
2018	GWN	AAA	23	1.03	1.99	3.10	0.9				
2018	NOR	AAA	23	0.84	3.38	5.31	0.0				
2018	ATL	MLB	23	1.58	8.53	5.71	-0.1	96.0	62.5	11.5	47.6
2018	BAL	MLB	23	2.44	18.56	9.68	-0.3	95.8	73	7	44.8
2019	NOR	AAA	24	1.31	3.86	3.82	0.9				
2019	BAL	MLB	24	1.86	6.43	4.63	0.2	96.2	66.3	13.2	47.3
2020	BAL	MLB	25	1.45	5.10	4.69	0.1	95.8	68.3	12.5	47.9

Baltimore Orioles 2020

Evan Phillips, continued

Pitch Shape vs LHH   **Pitch Shape vs RHH**

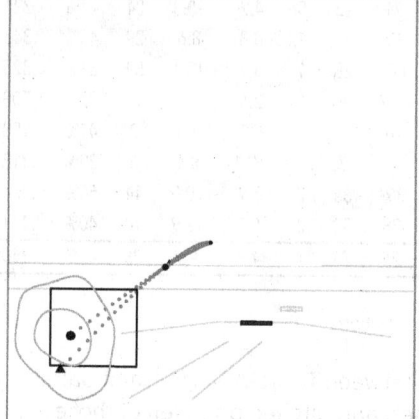
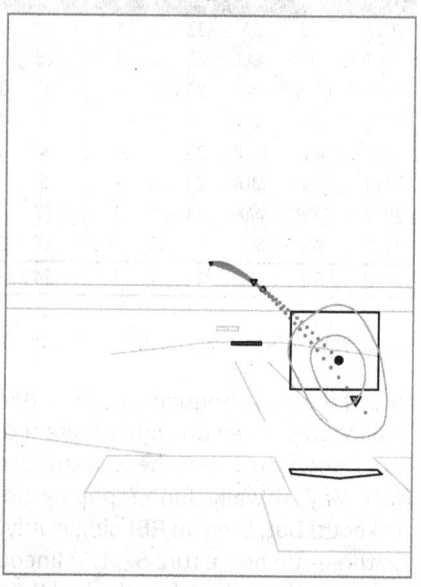

Type	Frequency	Velocity	H Movement	V Movement
● Fastball	65.1%	94.5 [106]	-8.7 [92]	-14 [105]
☐ Sinker				
+ Cutter				
▲ Changeup	7.7%	86 [103]	-9.4 [108]	-29.8 [93]
✕ Splitter				
▽ Slider	26.0%	85 [103]	6.5 [106]	-38.6 [84]
◇ Curveball				
◈ Slow Curveball				
✳ Knuckleball				
▼ Screwball				

Tanner Scott   LHP
Born: 07/22/94   Age: 25   Bats: R   Throws: L
Height: 6'2"   Weight: 220   Origin: Round 6, 2014 Draft (#181 overall)

YEAR	TEAM	LVL	AGE	W	L	SV	G	GS	IP	H	HR	BB/9	K/9	K	GB%	BABIP
2017	BOW	AA	22	0	2	0	24	24	69	45	2	6.0	11.3	87	54%	.281
2017	BAL	MLB	22	0	0	0	2	0	1^2	2	0	10.8	10.8	2	20%	.400
2018	NOR	AAA	23	0	1	0	10	0	12	10	0	6.8	9.8	13	62%	.345
2018	BAL	MLB	23	3	3	0	53	0	53^1	55	6	4.7	12.8	76	49%	.380
2019	NOR	AAA	24	3	4	7	30	0	45^1	35	2	3.0	11.3	57	56%	.303
2019	BAL	MLB	24	1	1	0	28	0	26^1	28	4	6.5	12.6	37	52%	.400
2020	*BAL*	*MLB*	*25*	*2*	*2*	*0*	*42*	*0*	*44*	*39*	*5*	*4.7*	*12.3*	*61*	*50%*	*.329*

Comparables: Rex Brothers, Hunter Wood, Edwin Díaz

"Just when they think they have the answers, I change the questions," said the late, iconic professional wrestler Roddy Piper. Minus the kilt, that about sums up Scott's 2019 season. He's still got a downhill fastball that topped out at 99 mph and a swing-and-miss slider on its day. And yet all he's ever been instructed to do is limit the walks and pitch in the zone. He did in his time at Triple-A this year, but opponents hit .479 with four home runs on pitches in the zone once he got to the big leagues, and of the 545 pitchers with at least 20 innings this year, only 19 walked more per inning. So Scott will enter his final option year with as much knowledge as anyone of the difference between just throwing it over and throwing quality strikes. It's just that not many of them throw 99 from the left side.

YEAR	TEAM	LVL	AGE	WHIP	ERA	DRA	WARP	MPH	FB%	WHF	CSP
2017	BOW	AA	22	1.32	2.22	3.24	1.6				
2017	BAL	MLB	22	2.40	10.80	2.36	0.1	100.2	70.3	10.8	29.6
2018	NOR	AAA	23	1.58	0.75	5.27	0.0				
2018	BAL	MLB	23	1.56	5.40	2.85	1.3	99.1	55.3	18	43.3
2019	NOR	AAA	24	1.10	2.98	2.44	1.7				
2019	BAL	MLB	24	1.78	4.78	4.52	0.2	98.2	58.8	15.5	42.8
2020	*BAL*	*MLB*	*25*	*1.41*	*4.45*	*4.07*	*0.5*	*98.5*	*58.2*	*17.4*	*40.6*

Baltimore Orioles 2020

Tanner Scott, continued

Pitch Shape vs LHH

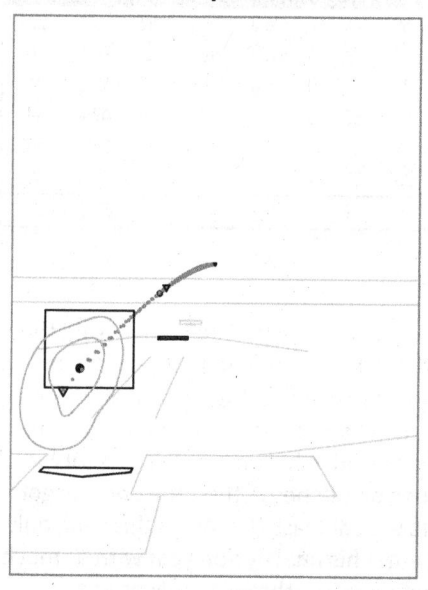

Pitch Shape vs RHH

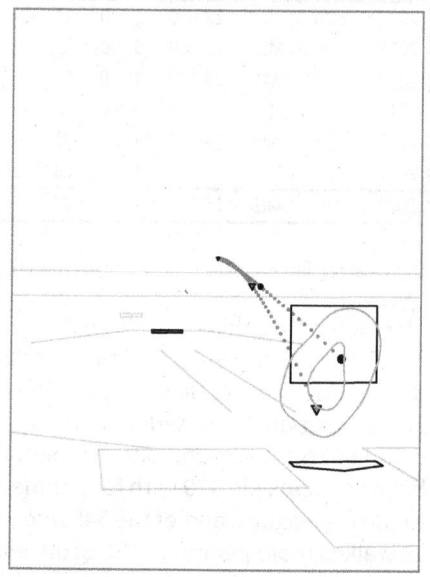

Type	Frequency	Velocity	H Movement	V Movement
● Fastball	55.7%	96.3 [111]	7.2 [99]	-15.1 [102]
□ Sinker	3.0%	95.6 [116]	12.8 [99]	-22.1 [94]
+ Cutter				
▲ Changeup				
✕ Splitter				
▽ Slider	41.3%	89.1 [120]	-3.6 [94]	-30 [109]
◇ Curveball				
◈ Slow Curveball				
✳ Knuckleball				
▼ Screwball				

Tayler Scott RHP
Born: 06/01/92 Age: 28 Bats: R Throws: R
Height: 6'3" Weight: 185 Origin: Round 5, 2011 Draft (#159 overall)

YEAR	TEAM	LVL	AGE	W	L	SV	G	GS	IP	H	HR	BB/9	K/9	K	GB%	BABIP
2017	BLX	AA	25	4	6	2	42	0	61^2	57	3	5.1	9.2	63	48%	.321
2017	ROU	AAA	25	0	1	1	12	0	13	17	3	3.5	9.0	13	52%	.341
2018	ROU	AAA	26	5	5	1	44	0	60^2	60	4	3.7	7.7	52	59%	.324
2019	TAC	AAA	27	3	2	1	20	0	35	32	4	4.9	12.1	47	56%	.350
2019	NOR	AAA	27	0	0	6	13	0	16	11	0	1.7	11.8	21	59%	.324
2019	SEA	MLB	27	0	0	0	5	2	7^2	11	1	7.0	8.2	7	65%	.400
2019	BAL	MLB	27	0	0	0	8	0	8^2	20	5	5.2	7.3	7	50%	.455
2020	BAL	MLB	28	2	2	0	33	0	35	41	6	4.0	7.3	28	53%	.319

Comparables: Marcus Hatley, Yacksel Ríos, Reed Garrett

If it isn't more complicated than this, then the rising sea levels will overtake Camden Yards before the Orioles are good again. It just seems like the team's driving force in major league player acquisition in 2019 was based on Triple-A stats, and the South African right-hander showed just how tenuous those can be. Scott didn't allow a run at Triple-A Norfolk from the time he was claimed on waivers to the last day of the season, spanning 13 appearances. In between, he made eight appearances for the Orioles and allowed runs in six of them for a double-digit ERA. On a major-league roster full of Triple-A pitchers, he showed that mostly drastically. But he did it with the best accent in the room.

YEAR	TEAM	LVL	AGE	WHIP	ERA	DRA	WARP	MPH	FB%	WHF	CSP
2017	BLX	AA	25	1.49	2.34	5.20	-0.3				
2017	ROU	AAA	25	1.69	7.62	5.59	0.0				
2018	ROU	AAA	26	1.40	3.26	4.62	0.4				
2019	TAC	AAA	27	1.46	6.43	3.61	0.9				
2019	NOR	AAA	27	0.88	0.56	1.80	0.7				
2019	SEA	MLB	27	2.22	9.39	5.65	0.0	96.7	51	13.8	44
2019	BAL	MLB	27	2.88	18.69	8.89	-0.3	96.1	61.2	7.2	45.4
2020	BAL	MLB	28	1.60	6.17	5.67	-0.2	95.8	57.4	9.9	45.1

Baltimore Orioles 2020

Tayler Scott, continued

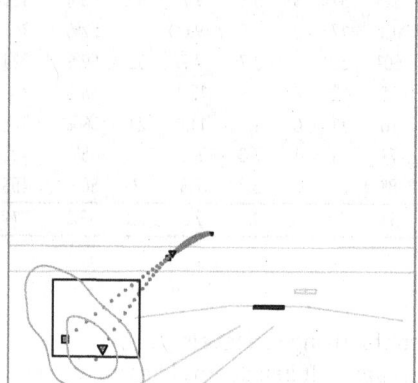
Pitch Shape vs LHH

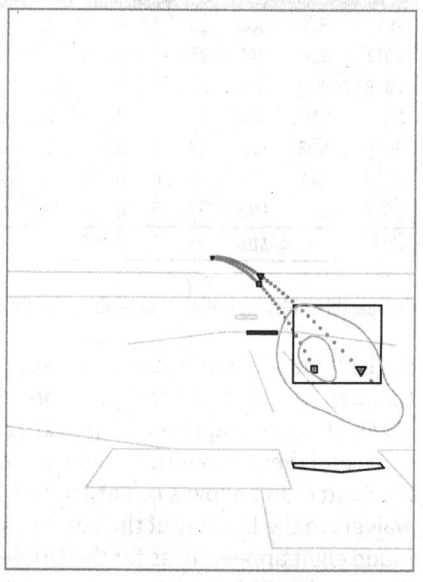
Pitch Shape vs RHH

Type	Frequency	Velocity	H Movement	V Movement
● Fastball	7.3%	95.3 [108]	-10 [86]	-15.7 [101]
□ Sinker	49.7%	94.7 [111]	-15.2 [83]	-21 [98]
+ Cutter				
▲ Changeup				
✕ Splitter				
▽ Slider	42.9%	89.2 [120]	4 [96]	-30.5 [108]
◇ Curveball				
◈ Slow Curveball				
✳ Knuckleball				
▼ Screwball				

Dillon Tate RHP

Born: 05/01/94 Age: 26 Bats: R Throws: R
Height: 6'2" Weight: 195 Origin: Round 1, 2015 Draft (#4 overall)

YEAR	TEAM	LVL	AGE	W	L	SV	G	GS	IP	H	HR	BB/9	K/9	K	GB%	BABIP
2017	TAM	A+	23	6	0	0	9	9	58^1	48	4	2.3	7.1	46	61%	.262
2017	TRN	AA	23	1	2	0	4	4	25	23	3	3.2	6.1	17	56%	.270
2018	TRN	AA	24	5	2	0	15	15	82^2	67	7	2.7	8.2	75	48%	.263
2018	BOW	AA	24	2	3	0	7	7	40^2	48	3	2.0	4.6	21	63%	.324
2019	BOW	AA	25	2	3	5	17	2	33^2	28	4	2.4	8.0	30	50%	.261
2019	NOR	AAA	25	2	0	2	4	0	9	7	1	1.0	7.0	7	65%	.240
2019	BAL	MLB	25	0	2	0	16	0	21	18	3	3.9	8.6	20	61%	.268
2020	BAL	MLB	26	1	1	0	18	0	19	20	3	3.3	7.7	16	54%	.301

Comparables: Yohan Pino, Zach Neal, John Means

How necessary was the move to the bullpen that Tate asked the Orioles' brass to give him after two starts this season? He allowed eight earned runs over those two starts, and allowed seven earned runs in 36 minor-league relief innings the rest of the way. His major-league debut wasn't a disaster, but his 93-96 mph sinker still doesn't miss bats. More consistent command of his slider and changeup could make Tate a viable middle reliever—an outcome that would seem like a success were he not drafted fourth overall in 2015 and traded twice before reaching it. Of course, the four pitchers the Orioles have selected with the fourth-overall pick this century have a median WARP barely north of one, so it's a low bar in Baltimore.

YEAR	TEAM	LVL	AGE	WHIP	ERA	DRA	WARP	MPH	FB%	WHF	CSP
2017	TAM	A+	23	1.08	2.62	3.46	1.2				
2017	TRN	AA	23	1.28	3.24	4.34	0.2				
2018	TRN	AA	24	1.11	3.38	4.77	0.6				
2018	BOW	AA	24	1.40	5.75	5.57	-0.1				
2019	BOW	AA	25	1.10	3.48	4.60	0.0				
2019	NOR	AAA	25	0.89	2.00	3.06	0.3				
2019	BAL	MLB	25	1.29	6.43	4.65	0.2	96.0	56.6	8.6	49.8
2020	BAL	MLB	26	1.43	5.29	4.83	0.1	95.6	57.6	8.7	50.7

Baltimore Orioles 2020

Dillon Tate, continued

Pitch Shape vs LHH

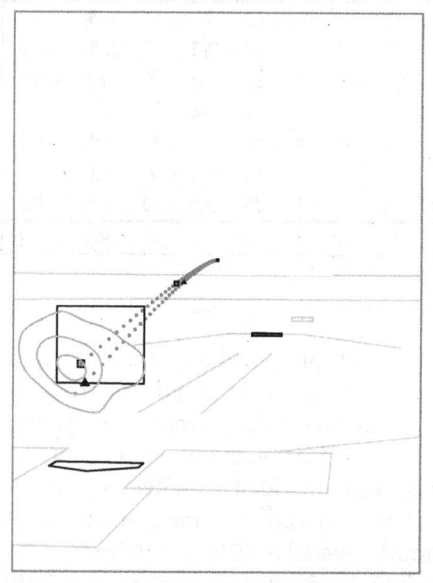

Pitch Shape vs RHH

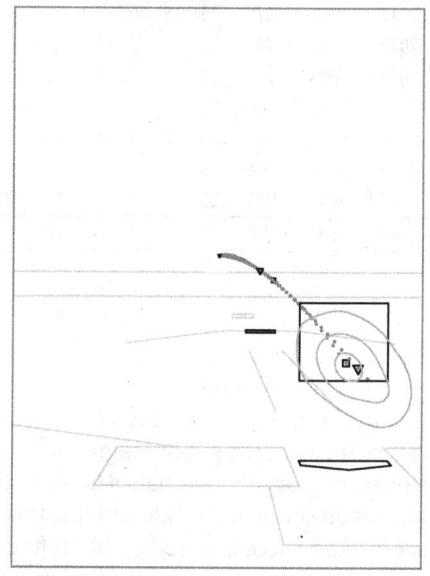

Type	Frequency	Velocity	H Movement	V Movement
● Fastball				
☐ Sinker	55.4%	94 [107]	-12.9 [98]	-22 [94]
+ Cutter				
▲ Changeup	19.1%	85.2 [100]	-12.9 [92]	-27 [101]
✕ Splitter				
▽ Slider	24.3%	84.9 [102]	5.1 [101]	-32.5 [102]
◇ Curveball				
◈ Slow Curveball				
✱ Knuckleball				
▼ Screwball				

Asher Wojciechowski RHP

Born: 12/21/88 Age: 31 Bats: R Throws: R
Height: 6'4" Weight: 235 Origin: Round 1, 2010 Draft (#41 overall)

YEAR	TEAM	LVL	AGE	W	L	SV	G	GS	IP	H	HR	BB/9	K/9	K	GB%	BABIP
2017	LOU	AAA	28	2	0	0	8	5	30²	24	2	2.3	10.3	35	28%	.275
2017	CIN	MLB	28	4	3	0	25	8	62¹	71	14	2.7	9.2	64	32%	.324
2018	NOR	AAA	29	5	4	0	19	12	84²	68	14	3.4	9.5	89	31%	.255
2018	CHR	AAA	29	0	5	0	6	6	34²	40	12	1.3	9.6	37	26%	.308
2019	COH	AAA	30	8	2	0	15	15	84²	67	19	3.3	8.7	82	28%	.227
2019	BAL	MLB	30	4	8	0	17	16	82¹	80	17	3.1	8.7	80	30%	.278
2020	BAL	MLB	31	7	9	0	35	23	126	124	29	3.1	8.2	116	29%	.275

Comparables: William Cuevas, André Rienzo, Chris Stratton

Considering that Wojcieshowski was a prospect coming up with the Houston Astros during the lean years of their rebuild, his coming full-circle as a 30-year-old, cash-purchased starter in this second-generation rebuild is being told to expect a four-course meal, only getting the salad, then being forced to do the dishes. It's not as though he didn't benefit from the modern game, though. Wojciechowski honed a breaking ball that looks like it was developed in a lab with the Cleveland Indians in spring training, embraced a long-toss program and pitched himself into a regular role in a major-league rotation. It will be his until the Orioles find someone homegrown to take it.

YEAR	TEAM	LVL	AGE	WHIP	ERA	DRA	WARP	MPH	FB%	WHF	CSP
2017	LOU	AAA	28	1.04	2.05	2.15	1.2				
2017	CIN	MLB	28	1.44	6.50	6.98	-1.1	94.2	61.8	11.3	48.9
2018	NOR	AAA	29	1.18	3.51	5.22	0.3				
2018	CHR	AAA	29	1.30	7.01	5.75	-0.1				
2019	COH	AAA	30	1.16	3.61	4.32	2.0				
2019	BAL	MLB	30	1.31	4.92	5.44	0.3	93.4	53.9	12.7	45.4
2020	BAL	MLB	31	1.34	5.35	4.96	0.8	92.8	56	12.2	46.4

Baltimore Orioles 2020

Asher Wojciechowski, continued

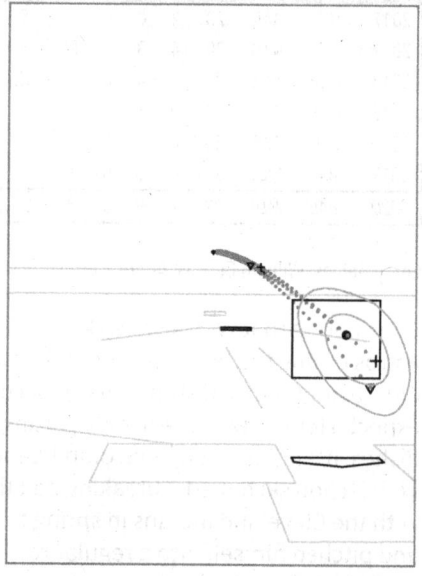

Type	Frequency	Velocity	H Movement	V Movement
● Fastball	53.9%	91.9 [98]	-3.1 [117]	-13.8 [106]
☐ Sinker				
+ Cutter	19.2%	86 [83]	5.4 [121]	-28.3 [84]
▲ Changeup				
✕ Splitter				
▽ Slider	24.6%	81 [85]	12.2 [130]	-39.1 [83]
◇ Curveball				
⊕ Slow Curveball				
✳ Knuckleball				
▼ Screwball				

98 - Orioles Player Analysis

Gabriel Ynoa   RHP

Born: 05/26/93   Age: 27   Bats: R   Throws: R
Height: 6'2"   Weight: 205   Origin: International Free Agent, 2009

YEAR	TEAM	LVL	AGE	W	L	SV	G	GS	IP	H	HR	BB/9	K/9	K	GB%	BABIP
2017	NOR	AAA	24	6	9	0	21	21	106^1	129	8	2.0	6.1	72	44%	.333
2017	BAL	MLB	24	2	3	0	9	4	34^2	39	5	2.1	6.8	26	39%	.318
2018	BOW	AA	25	0	0	0	2	2	7	6	1	0.0	7.7	6	45%	.263
2019	NOR	AAA	26	1	0	0	3	3	17	13	3	3.2	6.9	13	59%	.208
2019	BAL	MLB	26	1	10	0	36	13	110^2	126	29	2.1	5.4	67	47%	.273
2020	BAL	MLB	27	2	2	0	33	0	35	39	6	2.6	6.2	24	47%	.297

Comparables: Justin Nicolino, Enrique Gonzalez, José Ureña

As these pages have often noted, Ynoa can be pretty interesting. He joined the Orioles in April in a long-relief role and pitched well enough over the first few weeks that the local media essentially wanted him to transition into being a starter or the closer. A few more outings and he would have been in line to be the manager, or maybe even the mayor. Alas, he kept up what's been a career of inconsistency and somehow managed to throw 110 2/3 innings without a single one of them meaning anything. He was outrighted a second time this offseason, and you know the old saying. Outright me once, shame on you. Outright me twice, I'm going to pitch in Japan.

YEAR	TEAM	LVL	AGE	WHIP	ERA	DRA	WARP	MPH	FB%	WHF	CSP
2017	NOR	AAA	24	1.44	5.25	6.21	-0.6				
2017	BAL	MLB	24	1.36	4.15	5.82	-0.2	95.8	55.7	10.2	47.4
2018	BOW	AA	25	0.86	2.57	4.09	0.1				
2019	NOR	AAA	26	1.12	4.76	2.65	0.7				
2019	BAL	MLB	26	1.37	5.61	6.72	-1.4	95.5	56.5	10.1	48.9
2020	BAL	MLB	27	1.41	5.45	5.28	0.0	95.1	57	10.2	48.9

Baltimore Orioles 2020

Gabriel Ynoa, continued

Pitch Shape vs LHH

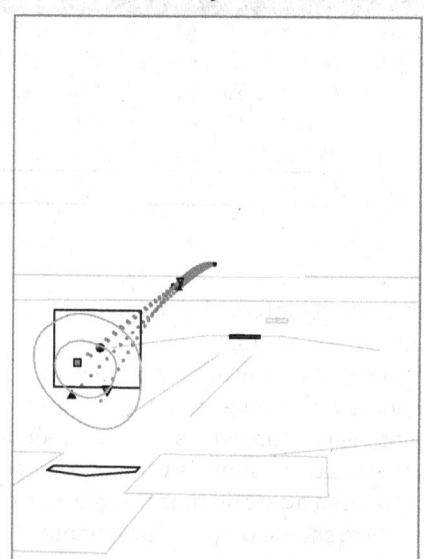

Pitch Shape vs RHH

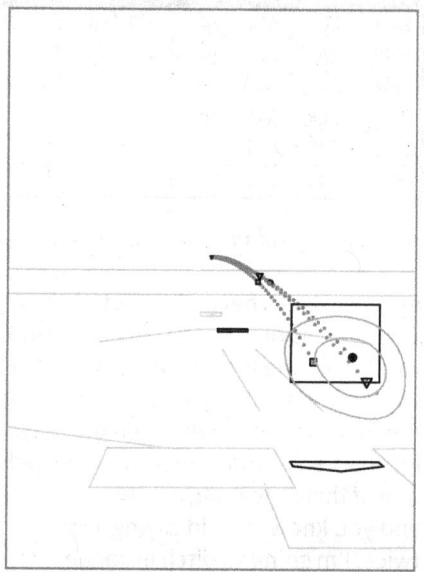

Type	Frequency	Velocity	H Movement	V Movement
● Fastball	27.9%	93.8 [104]	-10.8 [82]	-17.5 [96]
☐ Sinker	28.5%	93.9 [106]	-14.7 [87]	-20.9 [98]
+ Cutter				
▲ Changeup	13.2%	86.3 [104]	-14.9 [83]	-26.1 [104]
✕ Splitter				
▽ Slider	30.3%	84.1 [99]	2.6 [90]	-33.9 [98]
◇ Curveball				
⊕ Slow Curveball				
✱ Knuckleball				
▼ Screwball				

PLAYER COMMENTS WITHOUT GRAPHS

Taylor Davis C

Born: 11/28/89 Age: 30 Bats: R Throws: R
Height: 5'10" Weight: 200 Origin: Round 49, 2008 Draft (#1456 overall)

YEAR	TEAM	LVL	AGE	PA	R	2B	3B	HR	RBI	BB	K	SB	CS	AVG/OBP/SLG
2017	IOW	AAA	27	406	41	27	1	6	62	37	45	0	3	.297/.357/.429
2017	CHN	MLB	27	13	1	1	0	0	1	0	4	0	0	.231/.231/.308
2018	IOW	AAA	28	409	38	18	0	4	41	40	57	0	2	.275/.348/.360
2018	CHN	MLB	28	6	0	0	0	0	2	0	1	0	0	.400/.333/.400
2019	IOW	AAA	29	241	21	4	0	5	23	31	38	0	0	.235/.338/.328
2019	CHN	MLB	29	20	2	0	0	1	4	2	4	0	0	.167/.250/.333
2020	CHN	MLB	30	251	22	10	0	4	23	22	48	0	0	.222/.293/.327

Comparables: David Freitas, Jason Jaramillo, Manny Piña

Davis seemed destined to be remembered as the random minor-league backstop whose career-defining moment involved him staring at the camera a lot. We're delighted to report that changed in 2019, when he delivered an early-season grand slam to tie a contest against the Cardinals. The Cubs would then go on to win that game. We have to imagine Davis felt pretty good afterward. It'll have to last him, because he's probably not going to find himself on the glorious side of many more big-league moments.

YEAR	TEAM	P. COUNT	FRM RUNS	BLK RUNS	THRW RUNS	TOT RUNS
2017	CHN	70	0.0	0.1	0.0	1.0
2017	IOW	8301	12.7	0.0	-0.9	12.4
2018	CHN	51	0.0	0.0	0.0	1.5
2018	IOW	9120	9.8	0.3	-0.6	10.1
2019	CHN	702	0.5	-0.7	-0.1	-0.4
2019	IOW	7225	4.2	0.1	-0.8	3.5
2020	CHN	6850	2.6	-1.4	-0.3	0.9

YEAR	TEAM	LVL	AGE	PA	DRC+	VORP	BABIP	BRR	FRAA	WARP
2017	IOW	AAA	27	406	109	19.5	.318	-2.0	C(59): 11.9, 1B(26): -1.3	2.8
2017	CHN	MLB	27	13	68	-0.8	.333	-0.2	3B(2): 0.0, 1B(2): 0.0	0.0
2018	IOW	AAA	28	409	105	13.8	.315	-2.7	C(67): 8.1, 1B(24): -1.3	2.3
2018	CHN	MLB	28	6	90	0.5	.400	0.0	C(3): 0.1, 1B(1): 0.0	0.0
2019	IOW	AAA	29	241	82	1.7	.265	-2.4	C(51): 3.0, 1B(6): 1.1	0.8
2019	CHN	MLB	29	20	80	0.7	.154	0.1	C(6): -0.4, 1B(1): 0.0	0.1
2020	CHN	MLB	30	251	68	-2.8	.265	-0.6	C 1, 1B 0	-0.3

Baltimore Orioles 2020

Cadyn Grenier SS
Born: 10/31/96 Age: 23 Bats: R Throws: R
Height: 5'11" Weight: 188 Origin: Round 1, 2018 Draft (#37 overall)

YEAR	TEAM	LVL	AGE	PA	R	2B	3B	HR	RBI	BB	K	SB	CS	AVG/OBP/SLG
2018	DEL	A	21	183	23	12	2	1	13	17	53	3	2	.216/.297/.333
2019	DEL	A	22	364	49	18	3	7	39	48	107	5	1	.253/.360/.399
2019	FRD	A+	22	92	11	4	1	1	4	11	31	2	1	.208/.337/.325
2020	BAL	MLB	23	251	22	12	1	6	25	17	93	1	0	.208/.271/.342

Comparables: Michael Perez, Jeremy Hazelbaker, Jaylin Davis

The 2018 College World Series winners from Oregon State had plenty of offensive firepower that has translated into early pro success, perhaps most notably with the Orioles' top pick in 2019, Adley Rutschman. But as infielder Nick Madrigal put himself on the cusp of a major-league call with the White Sox and outfielder Trevor Larnach tore it up at the plate with the Twins system, Grenier barely lived up to his billing as a standout defender and excelled at little else in a difficult full-season debut. The 2018 competitive balance pick has a decent approach but no fluidity or power in his swing, and unless the Orioles can change that, it will have been a lot of draft capital spent on the type of player that can be had as a low-cost free agent or Rule 5 pick. They'd know. They grabbed a half-dozen last year.

YEAR	TEAM	LVL	AGE	PA	DRC+	VORP	BABIP	BRR	FRAA	WARP
2018	DEL	A	21	183	84	9.9	.312	-0.5	SS(39): 2.7	0.7
2019	DEL	A	22	364	123	29.3	.360	3.0	SS(54): 6.1, 2B(26): -2.2	2.9
2019	FRD	A+	22	92	72	2.4	.333	0.9	SS(22): 2.7	0.5
2020	BAL	MLB	23	251	62	-4.7	.321	-0.3	SS 4, 2B 0	-0.1

Ryan McKenna OF

Born: 02/14/97 Age: 23 Bats: R Throws: R
Height: 5'11" Weight: 185 Origin: Round 4, 2015 Draft (#133 overall)

YEAR	TEAM	LVL	AGE	PA	R	2B	3B	HR	RBI	BB	K	SB	CS	AVG/OBP/SLG
2017	DEL	A	20	530	62	33	2	7	42	43	128	20	2	.256/.331/.380
2018	FRD	A+	21	301	60	18	2	8	37	37	45	5	6	.377/.467/.556
2018	BOW	AA	21	250	35	8	2	3	16	29	56	4	1	.239/.341/.338
2019	BOW	AA	22	567	78	26	6	9	54	59	121	25	11	.232/.321/.365
2020	BAL	MLB	23	175	17	9	1	4	18	14	47	2	1	.226/.299/.367

Comparables: Brandon Nimmo, Brett Phillips, Rey Fuentes

McKenna took a massive step forward in 2018, but the indicators behind a 2019 in which he didn't make much progress aren't the kind that lend themselves to an undersized center fielder leaning into his skillset. McKenna bulked up last offseason and saw his fly ball rate jump to 40.3 percent, the highest it has been in full-season ball, while pulling the ball more than ever. That approach has led to unprecedented success for many, but McKenna strayed too far from the profile that has propelled him to the upper minors and onto prospect lists. There's no shame in being a plus defender at a premium position with a hose for an arm, who makes his bones offensively on his speed and ability to drive the ball into the gaps.

YEAR	TEAM	LVL	AGE	PA	DRC+	VORP	BABIP	BRR	FRAA	WARP
2017	DEL	A	20	530	117	28.3	.336	-0.2	CF(124): -7.6	1.8
2018	FRD	A+	21	301	218	46.2	.436	2.5	CF(64): -6.2, LF(2): -0.2	4.1
2018	BOW	AA	21	250	90	10.7	.312	2.6	CF(55): 3.4, RF(3): 2.1	1.4
2019	BOW	AA	22	567	112	21.5	.287	1.9	CF(98): -4.1, LF(18): 0.6	2.3
2020	BAL	MLB	23	175	76	0.8	.294	0.1	CF 0, LF 1	0.1

Baltimore Orioles 2020

Ryan Mountcastle 1B

Born: 02/18/97   Age: 23   Bats: R   Throws: R
Height: 6'3"   Weight: 195   Origin: Round 1, 2015 Draft (#36 overall)

YEAR	TEAM	LVL	AGE	PA	R	2B	3B	HR	RBI	BB	K	SB	CS	AVG/OBP/SLG
2017	FRD	A+	20	379	63	35	1	15	47	14	61	8	2	.314/.343/.542
2017	BOW	AA	20	159	18	13	0	3	15	3	35	0	0	.222/.239/.366
2018	BOW	AA	21	428	63	19	4	13	59	26	79	2	0	.297/.341/.464
2019	NOR	AAA	22	553	81	35	1	25	83	24	130	2	1	.312/.344/.527
2020	BAL	MLB	23	385	44	22	1	17	54	15	104	2	1	.266/.299/.472

Comparables: Brendan Rodgers, Richard Ureña, Justin Williams

Drafted as a shortstop in 2015 before tumbling down the defensive spectrum, Mountcastle has been held to a standard that often overlooks what he was taken 36th overall for: he can absolutely mash. The fact that he has loose, quick hands that can get to anything and has grown into significant power gets lost as he's penalized for his defensive outlook and whether he walks enough. Those concerns are legitimate, but they are also not going to be wished away by another tour in Norfolk. Look for the Orioles to talk them up following spring training as a defense (ha ha) of why Mountcastle isn't in Baltimore until all relevant service time and free agency dates have passed.

YEAR	TEAM	LVL	AGE	PA	DRC+	VORP	BABIP	BRR	FRAA	WARP
2017	FRD	A+	20	379	137	28.3	.343	1.5	SS(82): -12.1	1.8
2017	BOW	AA	20	159	56	-0.4	.265	0.5	3B(37): -1.1	-0.3
2018	BOW	AA	21	428	119	22.2	.339	-1.5	3B(81): -4.9	1.6
2019	NOR	AAA	22	553	115	18.2	.370	-0.9	1B(84): -6.1, LF(25): 2.1	1.3
2020	BAL	MLB	23	385	93	4.2	.326	-0.6	3B -2, 1B 0	0.2

Adley Rutschman C

Born: 02/06/98 Age: 22 Bats: B Throws: R
Height: 6'2" Weight: 216 Origin: Round 1, 2019 Draft (#1 overall)

YEAR	TEAM	LVL	AGE	PA	R	2B	3B	HR	RBI	BB	K	SB	CS	AVG/OBP/SLG
2019	ABE	A-	21	92	11	7	1	1	15	12	16	0	0	.325/.413/.481
2019	DEL	A	21	47	5	1	0	2	8	6	9	0	0	.154/.261/.333
2020	BAL	MLB	22	251	24	12	1	7	27	18	65	2	1	.219/.281/.363

Comparables: Lucas Duda, Chris McGuiness, Christian Walker

Someone goes 1-1 in the MLB draft every year, but few arrive with the expectations that Rutschman did as the Orioles' top pick in 2019. Not only is he the franchise savior and a second chance at a perennial All-Star catcher in Baltimore this century, but he gets to make nearly every stop of his minor league journey inside the state of Maryland, meaning there's no hiding any bumps in the road. Luckily for him, the Orioles don't expect there to be. He's an advanced defensive catcher with a plus arm and good receiving; he can be a 70 hitter with pop, and won't get himself out at the plate; one of his college coaches promised the local newspaper that he'd feed the hungry in Baltimore while extolling his virtues. It might be a couple years before he gets that chance, but rarely are there easier picks than the one the Orioles made in June.

YEAR	TEAM	LVL	AGE	PA	DRC+	VORP	BABIP	BRR	FRAA	WARP
2019	ABE	A-	21	92	177	11.5	.387	-0.1	C(9): -0.2	0.8
2019	DEL	A	21	47	85	1.2	.138	0.1	C(6): 0.1	0.1
2020	BAL	MLB	22	251	73	-0.7	.275	0.0	C 0	-0.1

Baltimore Orioles 2020

Dwight Smith Jr   LF

Born: 10/26/92   Age: 27   Bats: L   Throws: R
Height: 6'0"   Weight: 210   Origin: Round 1, 2011 Draft (#53 overall)

YEAR	TEAM	LVL	AGE	PA	R	2B	3B	HR	RBI	BB	K	SB	CS	AVG/OBP/SLG
2017	BUF	AAA	24	449	56	21	1	8	46	47	71	8	8	.273/.350/.392
2017	TOR	MLB	24	29	2	2	0	0	1	1	10	1	0	.370/.414/.444
2018	BUF	AAA	25	361	39	25	1	6	42	44	53	9	3	.268/.358/.413
2018	TOR	MLB	25	75	9	8	0	2	8	7	13	0	0	.262/.347/.477
2019	NOR	AAA	26	49	9	2	0	3	12	3	8	0	0	.311/.367/.556
2019	BAL	MLB	26	392	46	16	3	13	53	26	82	5	1	.241/.297/.412
2020	BAL	MLB	27	315	34	15	1	11	38	25	65	3	2	.241/.306/.411

Comparables: Bob Nieman, Stephen Piscotty, Aaron Cunningham

Acquired in a DFA trade from the Toronto Blue Jays, Smith essentially went from spending two years on a really talented Triple-A team with the likes of Vladimir Guerrero Jr., Rowdy Tellez and Danny Jansen to a more talented Triple-A team in big-league clothes. But what began as a possible breakout for Smith with a hot April ultimately cooled, and his OPS never got back above .800 after the end of May. Without the chance to make much defensive impact, Smith will need to start driving the ball more in order to keep getting opportunities in a crowded Orioles outfield at the corners. They moved Trey Mancini to right field to accommodate Smith in 2019; it's more likely Smith will move on to accommodate someone younger in left field in 2020 and beyond.

YEAR	TEAM	LVL	AGE	PA	DRC+	VORP	BABIP	BRR	FRAA	WARP
2017	BUF	AAA	24	449	117	14.8	.313	0.6	RF(67): -4.0, LF(32): -0.6	1.2
2017	TOR	MLB	24	29	69	2.8	.588	0.9	LF(9): -1.8, CF(1): 0.0	-0.2
2018	BUF	AAA	25	361	131	11.4	.302	-0.3	LF(62): 1.2, RF(14): -0.1	1.9
2018	TOR	MLB	25	75	99	3.7	.294	-0.4	LF(19): -1.5, RF(6): 0.7	0.1
2019	NOR	AAA	26	49	117	3.7	.324	-0.1	LF(5): -0.3, RF(2): 0.1	0.2
2019	BAL	MLB	26	392	82	1.0	.274	-0.1	LF(86): -0.7	0.0
2020	BAL	MLB	27	315	84	1.1	.278	-0.2	LF -1, RF -1	-0.1

Keegan Akin LHP

Born: 04/01/95 Age: 25 Bats: L Throws: L
Height: 6'0" Weight: 225 Origin: Round 2, 2016 Draft (#54 overall)

YEAR	TEAM	LVL	AGE	W	L	SV	G	GS	IP	H	HR	BB/9	K/9	K	GB%	BABIP
2017	FRD	A+	22	7	8	0	21	21	100	89	12	4.1	10.0	111	38%	.307
2018	BOW	AA	23	14	7	0	25	25	137^2	114	16	3.8	9.3	142	32%	.278
2019	NOR	AAA	24	6	7	0	25	24	112^1	109	10	4.9	10.5	131	34%	.331
2020	BAL	MLB	25	4	5	0	16	16	68	71	12	3.7	9.1	68	34%	.310

Comparables: Matt Hall, Brad Mills, Taylor Hearn

In his yard in Sumner, Michigan, Akin turned a pole barn into his own pitching facility to train in during the offseason, with mounds, a strike zone painted on a tarp, some weights and enough heat and electricity so that none of it's very spartan. It's enough to create easy solutions in Michigan winters, but might not be enough to turn him into the modern pitcher the Orioles want him to be. Perhaps an Edgertronic camera or Rapsodo system will help develop the inconsistent changeup and slider he'll need to be a backend starter for the Orioles. It's a role that his "invisiball" heater—sitting at 89-93 mph and eluding barrels—has him on the cusp of for 2020 and beyond.

YEAR	TEAM	LVL	AGE	WHIP	ERA	DRA	WARP	MPH	FB%	WHF	CSP
2017	FRD	A+	22	1.35	4.14	3.96	1.5				
2018	BOW	AA	23	1.25	3.27	3.76	2.5				
2019	NOR	AAA	24	1.51	4.73	4.36	2.6				
2020	BAL	MLB	25	1.45	5.29	4.88	0.5				

Baltimore Orioles 2020

DL Hall   LHP
Born: 09/19/98   Age: 21   Bats: L   Throws: L
Height: 6'2"   Weight: 195   Origin: Round 1, 2017 Draft (#21 overall)

YEAR	TEAM	LVL	AGE	W	L	SV	G	GS	IP	H	HR	BB/9	K/9	K	GB%	BABIP
2017	ORI	RK	18	0	0	0	5	5	10^1	10	1	8.7	10.5	12	58%	.360
2018	DEL	A	19	2	7	0	22	20	94^1	68	6	4.0	9.5	100	46%	.262
2019	FRD	A+	20	4	5	1	19	17	80^2	53	3	6.0	12.9	116	36%	.299
2020	BAL	MLB	21	2	2	0	33	0	35	35	5	4.2	10.5	41	39%	.327

Comparables: Jeremy Jeffress, Alex Reyes, Jesse Biddle

It's hard to figure what offseason development ahead of the 2019 season benefitted Hall more: the change in nomenclature that transformed the disabled list and its abbreviation to injured list, or the regime change in Baltimore that installed a staff with a background in bringing along young pitching. They have a great piece to work with in the 2017 first-round pick, whose fastball was up to 97 mph in a walk-laden year at High-A Frederick. He's still trying to get back the feel for his plus curveball he came out of high school with, but has developed an above-average changeup in the meantime. Fortunately for the Orioles, he went to the Futures Game and realized his stuff was too good to not throw in the zone. Hall re-affirmed his top-end rotation potential by throwing down a 2.67 ERA with 36 strikeouts against 12 walks between that appearance and an oblique injury that prematurely ended his season.

YEAR	TEAM	LVL	AGE	WHIP	ERA	DRA	WARP	MPH	FB%	WHF	CSP
2017	ORI	RK	18	1.94	6.97	6.58	-0.1				
2018	DEL	A	19	1.17	2.10	3.80	1.5				
2019	FRD	A+	20	1.33	3.46	3.72	1.3				
2020	BAL	MLB	21	1.47	5.16	4.89	0.1				

Nate Karns RHP

Born: 11/25/87 Age: 32 Bats: R Throws: R
Height: 6'3" Weight: 225 Origin: Round 12, 2009 Draft (#352 overall)

YEAR	TEAM	LVL	AGE	W	L	SV	G	GS	IP	H	HR	BB/9	K/9	K	GB%	BABIP
2017	KCA	MLB	29	2	2	0	9	8	45¹	41	9	2.6	10.1	51	48%	.283
2019	BAL	MLB	31	0	1	0	4	2	5¹	7	0	5.1	8.4	5	75%	.438
2020	BAL	MLB	32	2	2	0	33	0	35	33	7	4.1	7.3	28	40%	.263

Comparables: Tyson Ross, Mike Bolsinger, Blake Treinen

In the Year of the Home Run, no team allowed more than the Orioles, who broke the previous record of 256 allowed in August and ended the season with a grueling 305. The league as a whole saw 6,776 of them hit. On the Orioles alone, 36 pitchers allowed home runs—and three of them weren't even actual pitchers. But Karns stood alone having not allowed a home run in any of his four appearances. That he made just four appearances, as he dealt with forearm soreness all year and was released in August, means the Orioles' only offseason major-league free agent didn't do much to help any of their causes whether good or evil. That said, he made himself into the answer to the saddest trivia question ever conceived.

YEAR	TEAM	LVL	AGE	WHIP	ERA	DRA	WARP	MPH	FB%	WHF	CSP
2017	KCA	MLB	29	1.19	4.17	4.94	0.3	95.4	49.4	13.6	47.7
2019	BAL	MLB	31	1.88	0.00	4.38	0.1	93.8	65.9	11	45.5
2020	BAL	MLB	32	1.40	5.13	4.94	0.1	94.2	51.7	13	45.9

Baltimore Orioles 2020

Luis Ortiz   RHP
Born: 09/22/95   Age: 24   Bats: R   Throws: R
Height: 6'3"   Weight: 230   Origin: Round 1, 2014 Draft (#30 overall)

YEAR	TEAM	LVL	AGE	W	L	SV	G	GS	IP	H	HR	BB/9	K/9	K	GB%	BABIP
2017	BLX	AA	21	4	7	0	22	20	94^1	79	12	3.5	7.5	79	36%	.258
2018	BLX	AA	22	3	4	2	16	11	68	63	7	2.4	8.6	65	48%	.289
2018	NOR	AAA	22	2	1	0	6	6	31^2	34	4	2.3	6.0	21	40%	.297
2018	BAL	MLB	22	0	1	0	2	1	2^1	7	0	11.6	0.0	0	53%	.467
2019	NOR	AAA	23	3	7	0	14	14	66^1	77	15	4.2	6.4	47	47%	.294
2019	BAL	MLB	23	0	1	0	1	1	3^1	4	2	13.5	8.1	3	30%	.250
2020	BAL	MLB	24	2	2	0	33	0	35	38	6	3.8	5.6	22	43%	.289

Comparables: Zach Lee, Jake Thompson, David Holmberg

Ortiz's fall from being the Texas Rangers' first-round pick in 2014 to where he ended 2019 can be summed up in Brandon Hyde's six-word response when asked about the big righty making a spot start in June. "I have no idea what to expect," Hyde said, though that was only because he couldn't say what everyone has come to expect: a fastball that bumps up in the mid-90s but is imminently hittable, and nothing really to keep hitters off it. Until that changes, the answer to the question posed to Hyde won't be one the big right-hander wants to hear.

YEAR	TEAM	LVL	AGE	WHIP	ERA	DRA	WARP	MPH	FB%	WHF	CSP
2017	BLX	AA	21	1.23	4.01	4.45	0.8				
2018	BLX	AA	22	1.19	3.71	4.10	0.9				
2018	NOR	AAA	22	1.33	3.69	5.47	0.0				
2018	BAL	MLB	22	4.29	15.43	7.94	-0.1	94.3	59.1	9.1	41.8
2019	NOR	AAA	23	1.63	6.38	5.88	0.5				
2019	BAL	MLB	23	2.70	10.80	6.61	0.0	96.4	52.5	1.7	44.3
2020	BAL	MLB	24	1.51	5.58	5.27	0.0	95.5	57.3	5.3	44.5

Grayson Rodriguez   RHP

Born: 11/16/99   Age: 20   Bats: L   Throws: R
Height: 6'5"   Weight: 220   Origin: Round 1, 2018 Draft (#11 overall)

YEAR	TEAM	LVL	AGE	W	L	SV	G	GS	IP	H	HR	BB/9	K/9	K	GB%	BABIP
2018	ORI	RK	18	0	2	0	9	8	19^1	17	0	3.3	9.3	20	43%	.321
2019	DEL	A	19	10	4	0	20	20	94	57	4	3.4	12.4	129	45%	.262
2020	BAL	MLB	20	2	2	0	33	0	35	34	5	3.5	10.1	39	42%	.317

Comparables: Tyler Glasnow, Clayton Kershaw, Lucas Giolito

When the Houston Astros brass that turned around that franchise took over ahead of the 2012 season, they already had a few gems in their farm system to jump-start it. If Mike Elias and company do the same in Baltimore, the first-round pick from the year before they arrived will be regarded as one of those. Rodriguez posted the highest strikeout-per-nine rate of any teenager in full-season ball with at least 90 innings, and only five pitchers in all the minors at that threshold had a higher strikeout rate than his 34.2 percent. His big fastball—which was up to 98 mph and sits easily in the mid-90s—is a major reason why. But combine his fantastic starter's frame with the fact that he was able to develop a future plus changeup after learning it this spring, and there are many reasons the Orioles see a frontline starter in Rodriguez.

YEAR	TEAM	LVL	AGE	WHIP	ERA	DRA	WARP	MPH	FB%	WHF	CSP
2018	ORI	RK	18	1.24	1.40	2.89	0.7				
2019	DEL	A	19	0.99	2.68	2.69	2.8				
2020	BAL	MLB	20	1.37	4.66	4.51	0.3				

Baltimore Orioles 2020

Alex Wells LHP

Born: 02/27/97   Age: 23   Bats: L   Throws: L
Height: 6'1"   Weight: 190   Origin: International Free Agent, 2015

YEAR	TEAM	LVL	AGE	W	L	SV	G	GS	IP	H	HR	BB/9	K/9	K	GB%	BABIP
2017	DEL	A	20	11	5	0	25	25	140	118	16	0.6	7.3	113	43%	.251
2018	FRD	A+	21	7	8	0	24	24	135	142	19	2.2	6.7	101	36%	.301
2019	BOW	AA	22	8	6	0	24	24	137¹	123	10	1.6	6.9	105	43%	.274
2020	BAL	MLB	23	2	2	0	33	0	35	35	6	3.2	6.2	24	41%	.274

Comparables: Gabriel Ynoa, José Ureña, Paul Blackburn

Wells, a left-hander signed for $350,000 out of Australia in 2015 who has graduated from projectable to perplexingly effective with a fastball that tops out at 90 mph and impeccable command. He is one of 29 pitchers with at least 400 innings in the minors the last three years. He's in the top-five in WHIP (1.09), walks per nine (1.46), batting average against (.240) and ERA (2.92) among them. If you're going to put someone in the "prove it at every level" basket, there isn't much more one can do to prove it, though a fly-ball rate near 50 percent could be a dangerous proposition once he reaches Triple-A and the big leagues with the current baseball construction.

YEAR	TEAM	LVL	AGE	WHIP	ERA	DRA	WARP	MPH	FB%	WHF	CSP
2017	DEL	A	20	0.91	2.38	3.48	2.9				
2018	FRD	A+	21	1.30	3.47	5.21	0.2				
2019	BOW	AA	22	1.07	2.95	4.56	0.7				
2020	BAL	MLB	23	1.37	4.92	4.83	0.1				

LINEOUTS

Hitters

HITTER	POS	TEAM	LVL	AGE	PA	R	2B	3B	HR	RBI	BB	K	SB	CS	AVG/OBP/SLG	DRC+	WARP
Rylan Bannon	3B	NOR	AAA	23	90	18	10	0	3	17	3	14	0	1	.317/.344/.549	119	0.7
	3B	BOW	AA	23	444	45	22	4	8	42	47	72	8	4	.255/.345/.394	124	2.8
Yusniel Diaz	OF	FRD	A+	22	25	0	0	0	0	2	3	7	0	0	.273/.360/.273	88	-0.1
	OF	BOW	AA	22	322	45	19	4	11	53	32	67	0	3	.262/.335/.472	150	2.5
Adam Hall	SS	DEL	A	20	534	78	22	4	5	45	45	117	33	9	.298/.385/.395	140	4.5
Gunnar Henderson	SS	ORI	Rk	18	121	21	5	2	1	11	11	28	2	2	.259/.331/.370	65	0.0
Kyle Stowers	OF	ABE	A-	21	228	19	13	1	6	23	20	53	5	1	.216/.289/.377	88	0.5
Mason Williams	OF	NOR	AAA	27	494	62	15	3	18	67	46	86	4	7	.308/.371/.477	113	2.8
	OF	BAL	MLB	27	34	4	1	0	0	2	3	6	1	0	.267/.324/.300	93	0.1
Austin Wynns	C	NOR	AAA	28	230	26	5	0	3	25	25	35	0	0	.264/.351/.335	91	1.2
	C	BAL	MLB	28	74	8	1	0	1	5	3	14	0	0	.214/.247/.271	72	0.0

The wide-open stance that **Rylan Bannon** came to the Orioles with is now closed, but the equally-large gap in the bat-first infielder's defensive resume isn't. Bannon can play second base and third base and might have the pop to make an offensive impact at each, but the modern utility profile demands more. ⓧ **Yusniel Díaz**, the crown jewel of the Orioles' trade for Manny Machado in 2018, is entering Year Two of a staring match between a player whose fantastic tools seem destined to really only show themselves on a major-league stage and a front office who won't promote a player to said stage unless he's absolutely ready. ⓧ No player born in the Bahamas was ever selected in the MLB Draft before **Adam Hall** went in the second round of 2017, though he'd moved to Canada to pursue baseball long before that. It's not like there are many Canadian middle-infielders, either, but Hall's average-everything ceiling could change that as well. ⓧ There are three Gunnars ahead of 2019 second-round pick **Gunnar Henderson** in the race to be the first of his name to play in the big leagues, and three shortstops more advanced on the Orioles' depth chart for him to overtake to get there. The Orioles will be far more concerned with him accomplishing the latter than being the No. 1 Gunnar. ⓧ It's simple to get drafted on the first day when you are in the top five percent of average exit velocity for college hitters. **Kyle Stowers** will have to show he can get his bat on the ball enough for that easy plus raw power to be useful in right field. ⓧ There was a running joke around the Dan Duquette-led Orioles about his affinity for New England-born players and the sons of former Patriots (Hello, John Andreoli). **Mason Williams** joined the Orioles after Duquette was run out of town, and what's worse, he's actually useful as a spare outfielder. ⓧ Give credit where it's due: **Austin Wynns** has reached his ceiling as an up-and-down backup catcher with the Orioles. If he ever moves on from this organization, he can try to do it with a major-league team.

Baltimore Orioles 2020

Pitchers

PITCHER	TEAM	LVL	AGE	W	L	SV	G	GS	IP	H	HR	BB/9	K/9	K	GB%	WHIP	ERA	DRA	WARP
Brandon Bailey	CCH	AA	24	4	5	0	22	17	92^2	72	12	4.0	10.0	103	37%	1.22	3.30	4.18	0.8
Michael Baumann	FRD	A+	23	1	4	0	11	11	54	40	2	4.0	12.8	77	46%	1.19	3.83	3.79	0.8
	BOW	AA	23	6	2	1	13	11	70	45	2	2.7	8.4	65	43%	0.94	2.31	2.79	1.8
Marcos Diplan	PEN	AA	22	0	1	0	8	2	11	10	1	5.7	8.2	10	20%	1.55	4.09	6.38	-0.2
	BLX	AA	22	3	4	3	30	5	57^2	47	6	5.8	9.8	63	44%	1.46	4.99	5.55	-0.6
Ryan Eades	ROC	AAA	27	4	3	3	29	2	50^2	59	7	2.8	11.2	63	39%	1.48	5.51	5.16	0.5
	MIN	MLB	27	0	0	0	2	0	3^2	4	0	4.9	12.3	5	44%	1.64	0.00	5.23	0.0
	BAL	MLB	27	0	1	0	6	0	7^2	7	2	4.7	5.9	5	46%	1.43	3.52	5.74	0.0
Tom Eshelman	REA	AA	25	0	3	0	6	6	28^2	43	4	1.9	8.2	26	44%	1.71	6.28	7.01	-0.7
	NOR	AAA	25	2	1	0	7	6	38^1	43	6	1.6	6.6	28	45%	1.30	4.70	4.51	0.8
	LEH	AAA	25	1	1	0	4	4	26	23	3	1.7	8.0	23	49%	1.08	2.77	5.01	0.4
	BAL	MLB	25	1	2	0	10	4	36	47	12	2.8	5.5	22	33%	1.61	6.50	8.73	-1.2
Eric Hanhold	BIN	AA	25	2	0	2	9	0	14^2	9	1	3.1	11.0	18	50%	0.95	1.23	3.53	0.2
	SYR	AAA	25	3	4	0	39	0	48^2	59	5	3.9	6.7	36	49%	1.64	4.62	6.27	0.0
Dean Kremer	FRD	A+	23	0	0	0	2	2	9^2	6	0	3.7	13.0	14	20%	1.03	0.00	3.56	0.2
	BOW	AA	23	9	4	0	15	15	84^2	75	9	3.1	9.2	87	42%	1.23	2.98	4.68	0.3
	NOR	AAA	23	0	2	0	4	4	19^1	30	2	1.9	9.8	21	38%	1.76	8.84	7.58	-0.2
Zac Lowther	BOW	AA	23	13	7	0	26	26	148	102	8	3.8	9.4	154	41%	1.11	2.55	4.16	1.4
Josh Rogers	NOR	AAA	24	2	6	0	11	11	55	86	18	1.6	5.4	33	40%	1.75	8.51	8.40	-0.9
	BAL	MLB	24	0	1	0	5	0	14^1	18	7	3.8	3.1	5	24%	1.67	8.79	11.14	-0.9
Cody Sedlock	FRD	A+	24	4	1	0	13	10	61	38	4	3.8	9.7	66	42%	1.05	2.36	3.13	1.4
	BOW	AA	24	1	2	1	9	6	34	30	3	5.3	9.0	34	33%	1.47	3.71	5.75	-0.4
Chandler Shepherd	NOR	AAA	26	3	5	0	14	12	72^1	75	8	2.9	9.1	73	46%	1.35	4.60	6.19	0.3
	PAW	AAA	26	0	5	0	8	7	29^2	53	11	4.9	9.1	30	37%	2.33	10.01	5.94	0.2
	BAL	MLB	26	0	0	0	5	3	19	23	5	2.8	8.1	17	36%	1.53	6.63	7.27	-0.3
Kohl Stewart	ROC	AAA	24	8	6	0	20	19	91	90	10	4.4	7.9	80	53%	1.47	5.14	4.52	1.9
	MIN	MLB	24	2	2	0	9	2	25^1	29	5	2.8	3.6	10	49%	1.46	6.39	6.70	-0.3
Cole Sulser	DUR	AAA	29	6	3	2	49	4	66	51	4	3.3	12.1	89	32%	1.14	3.27	2.56	2.4
	TBA	MLB	29	0	0	0	7	0	7^1	5	0	3.7	11.0	9	35%	1.09	0.00	4.26	0.1
Bruce Zimmermann	BOW	AA	24	5	3	0	18	17	101^1	88	9	3.0	9.0	101	41%	1.20	2.58	4.38	0.7
	NOR	AAA	24	2	3	0	7	7	38^2	44	3	4.2	7.7	33	49%	1.60	4.89	5.69	0.4

Swiped from the Astros with the second pick in the Rule 5 draft, right-hander **Brandon Bailey** is an undersized starter who relies on a deep pitch mix and a solid changeup to survive. He'll also get you a third of the way to an Irish Car Bomb—something anyone watching the 2020 Orioles rotation figures to need. ⓘ No pitcher in the Orioles' system benefited more from their new philosophies than **Michael Baumann**, who threw a no-hitter a month into his time at Double-A Bowie. He has the makings of a plus slider and above-average changeup to go with his four-seam fastball that runs up to 99 mph. ⓫ If **Cody Carroll**'s back issue is resolved, he and his mid-to-upper-90s fastball might have avoided a fate worse than injury: pitching for the 2019 Orioles. ⓫ Teams seem to want **Marcos Diplan** enough to acquire him but not sufficiently so to keep him on their roster—he bounced from Milwaukee to Minnesota to Detroit and finally Baltimore within five months. A combination of prospect pedigree and the absence of any clear minor league progress may explain why. ⓫ It's easy to mock the Orioles for taking on everyone else's detritus, but former second-rounders like **Ryan Eades** are the types of risks Baltimore should be taking. ⓫ The statistics for **Tom Eshelman** are the product of an 85-mph fastball, fringe-average command, and an organization starved for any kind of pitching depth. ⓫ The Orioles' computer told them **Eric Hanhold**'s mid-90s fastball and ability to miss bats with his slider was worth a waiver claim, and that may prove to be true. The fact that they claimed him and sent him home rather than have him help a depleted pitching staff in September suggests otherwise. ⓫ **Dean Kremer** led the minors in strikeouts in 2018 with 178, and still struck out over a batter per inning in a 2019 shortened by a spring oblique strain. His plus curveball, fastball command and pitchability could make him one of the more successful young pitchers in the early phase of the Orioles rebuild when he debuts in 2020. ⓫ One of three pitchers with at least 150 strikeouts in the last two minor league seasons, **Zac Lowther** does it with a fastball in the 88-91 mph and a plus changeup. His elite extension makes everything play up. ⓫ **Josh Rogers** had UCL revision surgery—essentially a second Tommy John—in June. The whole arm contraption that came with it really took away from the drip. ⓫ Before the new Orioles' staff resurrected 2016 first-round pick **Cody Sedlock**'s career, it was laying on the operating table surrounded by the ghosts of Brian Matusz, Matt Hobgood and the cadre of Orioles' ruined pitching prospects. But for now, his career and fastball still have some life left. ⓫ Outrighting **Chandler Shepherd** the day after he started the final game of the season for the Orioles must have felt like a cigarette after an extremely regrettable romp. ⓫ **Kohl Stewart** is now 25, and he still hasn't figured out how to strike out anyone. It's … it's not an ideal outcome for the former fourth-overall pick. ⓫ **Cole Sulser** was a useful, two-pitch middle reliever in the Rays' organization in 2019. That means he will be a member of the Los Angeles Dodgers or the Milwaukee Brewers by the time the 2021 Annual goes to print. ⓫ Who has two thumbs, four pitches, a killer mustache and could arrive in Baltimore in 2020 to pitch in his hometown, saving the local media from writing about actual Orioles games for a week or so? **Bruce Zimmermann**.

Orioles Prospects

The State of the System
The 2020 Orioles system is much deeper than recent vintages, but it lacks impact talent beyond the first few names on the list below.

The Top Ten

★ ★ ★ *2020 Top 101 Prospect* **#4** ★ ★ ★

1
Adley Rutschman   C   OFP: 70   ETA: Early 2021
Born: 02/06/98   Age: 22   Bats: B   Throws: R   Height: 6'2"   Weight: 216
Origin: Round 1, 2019 Draft (#1 overall)

The Report: There isn't much he can't do on a baseball field. He has a beautiful swing that is basically identical from both sides of the plate. It's also a swing that's made for modern baseball with lots of loft, owing to quick hips and fast hands. His approach is a plus. He projects for plus or better game power. He pairs a catcher's frame with excellent athleticism. He's an average runner down the line—not an average runner for a catcher but an actual average runner. While he needs more reps calling games and handling professional baseball in general, he has all of the skills present to project as an excellent defensive catcher: hands, agility, arm, and perhaps most importantly, leadership. This is one of the best college position player prospects in recent memory, and he has a chance for some really big outcomes.

Variance: Low. There's always risk inherent to the tools of ignorance, and he didn't actually hit all that well coming off mono after his college season ended. Then again, he was coming off mono and his season started in February. It's extremely hard to see an outcome where he stays reasonably healthy and isn't at least a first-division starting catcher.

Mark Barry's Fantasy Take: The Pros: Great hitter, excellent plate discipline, 70 name.

The Cons: He's a catcher—that's kinda it.

This is one of the many "better in real life than fantasy" guys you'll find in this book. Rutschman is a top-25 dynasty guy, to be sure, and could easily be a top-three catcher in any format. He's still a catcher, though, which likely lowers his ceiling in comparison to other top-25 names.

Baltimore Orioles 2020

2 ★ ★ ★ 2020 Top 101 Prospect #45 ★ ★ ★

Grayson Rodriguez   RHP   OFP: 60   ETA: Late 2021
Born: 11/16/99   Age: 20   Bats: L   Throws: R   Height: 6'5"   Weight: 220
Origin: Round 1, 2018 Draft (#11 overall)

The Report: Imagine a big Texas prep pitcher who got picked pretty high in the first round last year. Your mental image is probably close enough for horseshoes here. Rodriguez started the season more in the low-to-mid 90s—occasionally scraping higher—but by the time the weather started cooling down again he was throwing hand grenades in the mid-to-upper 90s, frequently hitting 97 and 98. Rodriguez generates good plane and movement from his big frame. At various points in the season he showed the ability for three above-average-to-plus offspeed pitches. The slider was flashing as the best of these by the end of the season, a big sweeper in the low-80s that projects as a plus offering. The change more consistently projected as plus over the course of the full season, with strong dive and the potential to play pretty well in the same velocity band as the slider. The curve doesn't have a ton of velocity separation from the slider, leading to the potential for the pitches to run together in slurviness, but it has a nice shape to it on its own. Rodriguez also started throwing a cutter a tick or two on either side of 90 towards the end of the season, and that's a good pitch for his arm slot and arm speed. While the OFP here is technically the same as it was a year ago, it's gone from a soft 60 to a hard 60, and his chances of getting there have risen greatly as projectability becomes reality. If only 65 were a real grade…

Variance: Medium. There's inconsistency in his offspeed offerings. He's probably going to end up having to figure out which three pitches play best and work better on sequencing and tunneling; he's clustered his offerings from outing-to-outing and even inning-by-inning. There's all the general relief and durability risk you'd associate with a teenage pitcher here, too.

Mark Barry's Fantasy Take: With the regime change in Baltimore it's probably unfair to just type "Orioles pitcher LOL," which is certainly less fun. Even with the plague of his predecessors in mind, Rodriguez offers enough to potentially buck the trend. He's still a couple years away, but high-90s gas paired with a combo of potentially plus offspeed pitches is a perfect start to an SP2 upside.

3 ★ ★ ★ 2020 Top 101 Prospect #57 ★ ★ ★

Ryan Mountcastle   1B   OFP: 60   ETA: Early 2020
Born: 02/18/97   Age: 23   Bats: R   Throws: R   Height: 6'3"   Weight: 195
Origin: Round 1, 2015 Draft (#36 overall)

The Report: He just keeps hitting while sliding down the defensive spectrum. We don't usually describe right-handed swings as pretty, and while Mountcastle's swing may not get an exhibit in The Prado, he might hit like Martin. Mountcastle has plus bat speed, and can make loud contact in all four quadrants of the zone. He does tend to expand a bit too much, leading to a higher K-rate and lower quality of contact than you'd prefer in your bat-first prospect, but assuming some continued adjustments, it's an easy plus hit tool. Mountcastle always had a plus raw power projection, but found the Triple-A baseball particularly to his liking, knocking 35 doubles and 25 bombs in about three-quarters of a full season. That's about where I'd peg his potential major league production, but he will need to temper the approach to get to that level of pop in *Las Grandes Ligas*. That's a bit better than Martin Prado I suppose. It will need to be since we've made it 150 words into this blurb and haven't mentioned his glove yet. Mountcastle is finally, officially a first baseman. He's fine there.

Variance: Medium. The phrase "we really think Mountcastle will hit" may have been written more times than any other sequence of words at Baseball Prospectus over the last couple years (other than, perhaps, "the ball is juiced"). The Triple-A performance as a 22-year-old is nothing to sneeze at, even with the rabbit ball, but the aggressive approach may cause Mountcastle issues in the majors, barring an adjustment. And he's going to have to hit a lot.

Mark Barry's Fantasy Take: Last year, Ben comped Mountcastle to Nicholas Castellanos, and while I'd love nothing more to come up with a perfect replacement example of Mountcastle's future prospects, Castellanos just feels too right. The downgrade on the positional spectrum hurts a touch, but only a touch.

4 DL Hall   LHP   OFP: 60   ETA: Late 2021
Born: 09/19/98   Age: 21   Bats: L   Throws: L   Height: 6'2"   Weight: 195
Origin: Round 1, 2017 Draft (#21 overall)

The Report: Hall may have been lapped by Grayson Rodriguez as the organization's best pitching prospect, but that has more to do with the latter's excellence than the former's performance. Hall matched his success as a teenager in the Sally League with an equally impressive campaign as a 20-year-old in the Carolina League, and bettered it measuring by some of the peripherals. He was on pace to surpass his debut innings total when he was shelved with a lat strain in mid-August. The 2017 first-rounder's best pitch is undoubtedly his fastball, which sits 94-96 touching 97 and explodes up in the zone, carrying enough life when lower to still get swings and misses or weak contact. His low-80s curveball features good depth and sharp bite. It's his best secondary, and he can use it in any count. It's equally effective getting called strikes early to set up the fastball or as a put-away pitch down and glove-side.

Hall rounds out the mix with a better-than-decent change and the occasional slider. He's altered his approach this season to be more curve-heavy, and his K rate has jumped to nearly 13 per 9. He did have problems with his control that are worth tempering enthusiasm going forward, but Hall is athletic and the delivery is simple enough that he should have the ability to improve his command. All in all he's the same high-end mid-rotation starter prospect with high reliever risk that he was last year. Hall is going to contribute one way or another in the big leagues some day, but if it is going to be as a starter there are still some hurdles to clear.

Variance: Medium. He's got impact stuff from the left side but runs into issues with control and command that can look like markers of a move to the bullpen. Hall has a strong build and an athletic motion, but isn't tall, it isn't the prototypical pitcher's build, and he just went down with a season-ending lat injury. There's a lot that could happen in either direction, but it is tough to complain about his stuff or performance so far, and he's a 21-year-old ticketed for Double-A.

Mark Barry's Fantasy Take: There's something about Hall that just screams (how do I not say poor man's?) less-advantaged Robbie Ray. In a sense, that's great news for the O's. On the other hand, Ray never walked as many guys in the minors as Hall has. There's upside, yes, but as always, it comes with flame-out/relief potential.

5. Ryan McKenna OF

OFP: 55   ETA: Late 2020
Born: 02/14/97   Age: 23   Bats: R   Throws: R   Height: 5'11"   Weight: 185
Origin: Round 4, 2015 Draft (#133 overall)

The Report: McKenna's top line numbers as a 22-year-old in the Eastern League don't look amazing, but he heated up in the second half, and there's no real weakness on the scouting sheet. McKenna generates sneaky pop from minimal load and length, although he can get a bit pull-happy at times, which I suspect will limit the hit tool to average at the highest level. When he stays back and takes what he's given, he can drive the ball to the opposite field gap as well. There's the potential for 30-40 doubles in the profile, and McKenna should see enough fastballs on the inner half which he can yank to add double-digit home run totals to the back of his baseball card most years. He's a plus runner and should hold the speed, so while he's unlikely to challenge for Gold Gloves in center field, he's at worst average there. The only tool that doesn't grade out at least as a 5 is his arm, which is fringe, but accurate. There's not really a carrying tool in the profile though, and if McKenna doesn't temper his approach in the majors he may end up more as a fourth/extra outfielder.

Variance: Medium. The speed/glove up-the-middle gives him at least a bench outfielder downside projection, but he hasn't really hit in Double-A as much as you'd like to project an average hit tool. Don't scout that stat line, but the stat line indicates some approach/aggression issues that will need to be ironed out before McKenna can be a regular in the majors.

Mark Barry's Fantasy Take: Welcome to the first of many "Let's See What Happens With the Ball" guys, as McKenna likely won't really pop unless he adds a little, uh, power. The whole is greater than the sum of the parts, and McKenna does everything kinda/sorta well on the field. His proximity to the big leagues makes him an interesting dude in deeper formats, but the ceiling is relatively low here.

6. Yusniel Díaz OF
OFP: 55   ETA: Late 2020
Born: 10/07/96   Age: 23   Bats: R   Throws: R   Height: 6'1"   Weight: 195
Origin: International Free Agent, 2015

The Report: Díaz was the prospect centerpiece of the Manny Machado trade last summer, but a year-plus later it's not a slam dunk he'll end up the best major-league piece in the deal. Díaz missed almost all of May with an undisclosed injury, and then dealt with a quad issue late in the season. When he was on the field, he didn't dominate Double-A like you'd hope a top-50 prospect corner bat would. The raw pop is certainly still there. Díaz is strong enough, and has enough of an idea what pitches to drive, that you can still dream on 25-plus bombs in the majors. However, the swing has gotten stiffer and more grooved, leading to more bad contact in the zone. Everything looks a bit less athletic in the box this year, and Díaz's body has gotten a bit softer as well. He's still perfectly fine in right field, but that won't mean much if the bat doesn't carry its weight. You can still wishcast a .260 or .270 hitter with 25 bombs in a couple years, but Díaz now looks less like he will play up past the sum of his solid-average tools, and more like, well…maybe Stephen Piscotty?

Variance: Medium. Díaz and McKenna make a nifty side-by-side for this list. Díaz has more upside if the power plays in the majors, but he's less likely to sustain a major-league career if the hit tool lands at a 40 or 45. He's generally performed better in the minors though, so the risk factor ends up about the same, even though the shape of the risk is very different. Basically we think Díaz has less margin for error with the bat, but is less likely to just not hit at all.

Mark Barry's Fantasy Take: It's a little concerning that Díaz was more or less "fine" last season at Double-A Bowie and didn't really sniff a promotion to Norfolk, let alone Baltimore. Díaz isn't a write off by any means (.270 and 25-30 homers is still the ceiling), but the reports are trending in the wrong direction for him to live up to the Top Prospect in the organization billing he enjoyed just a year ago. He's basically variance-edition Ryan McKenna.

7. Adam Hall 2B/SS
OFP: 50   ETA: 2022
Born: 05/22/99   Age: 21   Bats: R   Throws: R   Height: 6'0"   Weight: 170
Origin: Round 2, 2017 Draft (#60 overall)

The Report: There's been a lot of excitement up to this point on this list. This year's 1.1! First-round pitchers with big arms! Toolsy hitters! Well, Adam Hall will…not be one of those reports. He's a good prospect, don't get me wrong. He's a solid, professional hitter. He's got solid bat-to-ball ability and drives the ball into the gaps a bit. He's got a solid approach and wasn't overmatched at all in an aggressive full-season assignment in his first full season as a Canadian prep.

Baltimore Orioles 2020

He's a solid defender in the middle infield with solid actions. You've probably noticed by now that I've used solid five times in the last four sentences, and you've probably correctly inferred there isn't anything particularly flashy here. There isn't huge tools upside anywhere in the profile, and he's more polished than projectable. But the guy with all of the 5s and 55s on the report and good performance is a good prospect too, even if he's terribly unlikely to ever bust out into a superstar. He is, in a word, solid.

Variance: Medium. This profile depends a lot on the hit tool projection, and the hit tool is one of the hardest things to project in A-ball hitters, generally. The rest of the skills are low variance.

Mark Barry's Fantasy Take: Hall's calling card for fantasy relevance will be his speed (he swiped 33 bags last season), but he'll need to be able to hit for the speed to play. I'm not overly optimistic that will happen. There are visions of a (way) less fast, less efficient Billy Hamilton dancing in my head, and that makes Hall a little less solid for fantasy purposes.

8. Dean Kremer   RHP
OFP: 50   ETA: 2020
Born: 01/07/96   Age: 24   Bats: R   Throws: R   Height: 6'3"   Weight: 180
Origin: Round 14, 2016 Draft (#431 overall)

The Report: Kremer has continued to dominate since his conversion back to starting pitching in 2018. Ironically, the success has come mostly because of his reliance on his two best pitches. Kremer's fastball sat in the mid-90s during his days as a reliever. It's more low-90s as a starter, but it has some nice plane and batters tend to see it late due to a deceptive arm action. He can pop it up in the zone effectively, which pairs well off his mid-70s curveball with 12-6 dive. It's not a true power breaker at that velocity band, but it's an effective pitch with an above-average projection. Kremer does show occasional issues moving it east-west in the zone, and will twist it off or use a bit of head whack to get it glove-side against righties. That would be less of an issue if his slider were more consistent, but the mid-80s offering tends to cut and ride up, lacking true two-plane movement. He has a straight change in the same velo band that he sells well, but tends to be overly firm. If Kremer can refine his third and fourth offerings a bit more, there's potential for a league-average starter here, but there might be more upside in seeing if he can find mid-90s velocity in the pen again and let him pair that with the above-average curve in a late-innings role.

Variance: Low. He has two quality major-league offerings in his repertoire already, now it's just a matter of what role he ends up in.

Mark Barry's Fantasy Take: Going out on a limb here, but I've always liked Kremer a little bit. He's still under-the-radar enough where you can keep him on the watch list for now, but you should definitely nab him if he can start to loosen up that change.

9. Michael Baumann RHP
OFP: 50   ETA: 2020
Born: 09/10/95   Age: 24   Bats: R   Throws: R   Height: 6'4"   Weight: 225
Origin: Round 3, 2017 Draft (#98 overall)

The Report: Everyone's favorite doppelgänger of everyone's favorite *Ringer* writer jumped from personal cheeseball to a real prospect arm in 2019. An improved changeup and slider give him four fringe-to-average offerings, and Baumann has a frame built to log innings in a major-league rotation. There's some effort in the delivery to get the fastball up to 95—and some outings he will sit more low 90s—but it shows good life above the hands due to his over-the-top slot. Down in the zone the heater can run a bit true, although he occasionally bores it in on lefties. Accidental cut? Who's to say nowadays.

The slider can run from slurvy to cutterish, but the Goldilocks-approved version around 85 has sharp two-plane action. Baumann's true curveball is a bit soft in the mid 70s, but the 12-6 downer action gives a different breaking ball look. His change can vacillate as well between circle and split action, but he's comfortable throwing it against lefties and sells the offering well enough for it to be more than a show-me pitch. Baumann might lack a true out pitch in the majors, making him more of a swingman or middle reliever, but the improving secondaries give him a shot to stick in the back of a rotation.

Variance: Low. There's not much left to project in the frame or the stuff, and there might not be sustained major league success in the rotation, but Baumann doesn't have much left to prove in the minors either.

Mark Barry's Fantasy Take: DRA might like Baumann more than Kremer, but a range of outcomes such as fringy starter, swingman and middle reliever doesn't inspire a ton of confidence for our purposes. So I guess, Orioles pitcher LOL (old habits die hard).

10. Cadyn Grenier SS
OFP: 50   ETA: 2021
Born: 10/31/96   Age: 23   Bats: R   Throws: R   Height: 5'11"   Weight: 188
Origin: Round 1, 2018 Draft (#37 overall)

The Report: He's *really* good defensively. Good enough that he pushed Nick Madrigal to second at Oregon State. Good enough that he mostly pushed Hall—a better prospect—to second when they were together in Delmarva. Good enough that he was a first-rounder last year even with critical questions about his hitting ability. Suffice to say, those questions remain. Grenier has some bat speed and pop, so he's not hopeless on offense. But he chases too much and doesn't adjust his bat path well, which leads to the potentially-fatal combination of too much swing-and-miss and too much poor contact when he does connect. As hinted at above, he can really go pick it at both short and second, so there's a high "floor" in that he should at least have some sort of utility player career even if he fails to hit much. He could probably be that already, frankly. There's just enough hitting ability to get him to a regular at present if you're optimistic, and, given the secondary abilities and general baseball feel, you can hope it gels if you're extremely optimistic. We're always known for our optimism here at the Baseball Prospectus Prospect Team, right?

Variance: Medium. He's very likely to make the majors and have a real career given his versatility, but there's a lot of room between the lower-side realistic outcomes where he's an up-and-down sixth infielder type and the OFP.

Mark Barry's Fantasy Take: Grenier is a great choice if your league only awards points for defensive stats or variations of the -adyn, -aydan, -aiden forename.

The Next Ten

11 Gunnar Henderson SS
Born: 06/29/01   Age: 19   Bats: L   Throws: R   Height: 6'3"   Weight: 195
Origin: Round 2, 2019 Draft (#42 overall)

Henderson, the Orioles second-round pick, got Mark Vientos comps around draft time. I can kind of see it physically, and he has the same kind of length to his swing, but without the same present raw that Vientos had as a teenager due to a pretty flat swing plane. There's better present athleticism, although Henderson might slide over to third himself as he fills out, and his actions can be a bit sluggish for the 6. He was also a youngish prep draftee, so he might eventually catch up to Vientos on the pop with some added strength and a swing tweak. It's an intriguing tool set overall, but 2020 will give us more data on what exactly the shape of the player might look like in a few years. For now, there's a major league OFP somewhere on the left side of the infield, but a much higher variance than even the upper-minors arms above him.

12 Austin Hays OF
Born: 07/05/95   Age: 24   Bats: R   Throws: R   Height: 6'1"   Weight: 195
Origin: Round 3, 2016 Draft (#91 overall)

Austin Hays. Boy, I don't know. Some players just peak at 21. That neat parabola arcing at Age 26-28 is a composite of thousands of player's careers. So it's not impossible the best season of his career came when he was torching a couple minor league levels. There were of course the two years of injuries that followed—ankle, thumb, hamstring—and rumors that the previous administration weren't as high on Hays as the prospect list makers were. He's been a beneficiary of the giant reset button in Charm City and found himself with a second chance to make a September impression. Hays has always been more of a broad base of skills type rather than an outfielder with a clear carrying tool, so there is the risk that the injuries may have eroded those skills to fringy. He's also never *really* hit above Double-A. On the other hand, it's a potential average hit/power profile and the ability to battle center field to a draw some days. Hays is not the trickiest "prospect" on this list to rank—that's still to come—but he has the weirdest variance profile in this glut of OFP 50 names.

13 Keegan Akin LHP
Born: 04/01/95 Age: 25 Bats: L Throws: L Height: 6'0" Weight: 225
Origin: Round 2, 2016 Draft (#54 overall)

It was more of the same for Akin this season, for good and ill. He gave back a tick or so of the mid-90s heat that popped up in 2018, but he still touches 95 with boring action in on righties, and can vary the fastball look with two-seam action in the low-90s. He has difficulty repeating his arm path, though, and continues to struggle with command and control of the fastball. The raw velocity from the left side, plus some deception, allows him to get swings and misses with the fastball, which is good because both secondaries remain below-average. He throws his low-80s slider a fair bit now, but it tends to slide down barrels rather than miss bats due to a lack of depth, and general slurviness. The 2019 Orioles used 40 pitchers in 2019 and Akin is likely to be one of the multitudes in 2020, but he's more likely to fit as a reliever than a starter.

14 Alex Wells LHP
Born: 02/27/97 Age: 23 Bats: L Throws: L Height: 6'1" Weight: 190
Origin: International Free Agent, 2015

I see—conservatively—two dozen different "soft-tossing lefties" over the course of the season, and I'll be the first to admit that I like Wells more than I should. I liked him more when he topped out at 90 in the Penn League though. It was 88 this year, but he manipulates the pitch well and will sink or cut it. There's 70 control and 60 command to boot. His best secondary is an average changeup that he throws a lot. It doesn't have ideal velocity separation, sitting in the low 80s, but there's enough late fade to miss bats or induce weak contact. I'd like him more if I could really get it to a plus projection, but for as much as he throws it there's too many hittable ones. He shows a slider and a curve. I actually prefer the slider as a left-on-left option, as his low-70s curve tends to be a bit loopy and obvious out of the hand. But the curve comes in from an incredibly difficult angle as Wells releases everything from as close to first base as possible for a southpaw with a relatively high slot. Despite the funk and crossfire, Wells is just playing catch out there and repeats everything well. I just wish the everything popped off the scouting sheet a little bit more. I'm not gonna bet against him doing enough to be a backend starter, but he looks more like a swingman or crossover lefty pen arm.

15 Zac Lowther LHP
Born: 04/30/96 Age: 24 Bats: L Throws: L Height: 6'2" Weight: 235
Origin: Round 2, 2017 Draft (#74 overall)

Baltimore Orioles 2020

You can shake up the names of the lefty arms in the Next Ten in a tombola and draw them out at random and I'd mostly shrug and then sign off on the results. Lowther has a better fastball than Wells in that he more regularly touches 90-91. He offers late, almost wiffle ball, movement on the pitch, along with even more deception, but less command. It's a tough angle for lefties, and Lowther has some success boring both the fastball and the change in on righties. The change is firm in the low 80s, but has enough fade to be effective, and Lowther can spot it to either side. He has two below-average breaking balls in the arsenal as well. There was internal discussion around the idea that a dude with that kind of natural fastball movement should be able to pick up some kind of breaking ball or cutter with a bit of "pitch design," but we also can't really project that. What we can project is another lefty swingman or fifth starter type.

16 Rylan Bannon   IF
Born: 04/22/96   Age: 24   Bats: R   Throws: R   Height: 5'7"   Weight: 180
Origin: Round 8, 2017 Draft (#250 overall)

Bannon doesn't have the slick glove of Grenier, the overall up-the-middle tool set of Hall, or the amateur pedigree of either. What he has done is hit at every level, showing surprising pop from an undersized frame. There won't be the 20+ home run power he showed in Rancho, because that's Rancho, but it's better-than-average raw, and he has the ability to stand at a few different infield spots (and could likely hack it in corner outfield as well). Yes, it's a grindy, Day 2 college bat that can't play a premium defensive spot. But Bannon doesn't have much left to prove in the minors, and while issues with spin might limit him to an extra infielder role, sometimes these guys show enough secondary skills that the whole profile plays up despite below-average batting averages.

17 Hunter Harvey   RHP
Born: 12/09/94   Age: 25   Bats: R   Throws: R   Height: 6'3"   Weight: 175
Origin: Round 1, 2013 Draft (#22 overall)

What a long, strange trip it has been. Hunter Harvey remains—much to my consternation—both still eligible for this list and functionally impossible to rank. He finally made his major-league debut in 2019. This comes after three years as a Top 101 arm which ended halfway into six injury-plagued minor league seasons where he threw just 250 innings total. Harvey is strictly a reliever now, but he's pumping 99 mph fastballs and a power curve to go with it. So it's badass late-inning stuff. He also was used sparingly in September because of "soreness." If the health record were a little better and the fastball a little less true he'd be a top 10 prospect in the system, but there's little evidence Harvey can handle even a 50-inning-a-year reliever workload at this point.

18 — Bruce Zimmermann LHP
Born: 02/09/95 Age: 25 Bats: L Throws: L Height: 6'2" Weight: 215
Origin: Round 5, 2017 Draft (#140 overall)

Zimmerman slides from 11 to 18 due to an improving system, but this southpaw varietal more or less held serve in 2019. He conquered Double-A the second time around, missing bats consistently with a sneaky fast ~90 mph heater and potentially average change. The change shows tight, late fade, and Zimmerman sells it well with the arm action. Is this starting to sound a lot like Zac Lowther? Well, sure. Zimmerman's slider is a tick better than Lowther's breaking balls—inconsistent, but flashing razorblade action in the low 80s. There's a humpy, low-70s curve as well, for a different look or to steal a strike. If you preferred Zimmerman over Lowther—or frankly some of the other arms in the Next Ten—that'd be fine by us, but the 24-year-old senior sign is more or less what he is right now, and Triple-A and the majors might be a bit rude to the profile.

19 — Drew Rom LHP
Born: 12/15/99 Age: 20 Bats: L Throws: L Height: 6'2" Weight: 170
Origin: Round 4, 2018 Draft (#115 overall)

Rom was quite solid in his full-season debut in the South Atlantic League. This was an aggressive assignment for a 19-year-old, fourth-round prep arm. Rom thrived with a four-pitch mix he can throw for strikes, including a solid slider. The fastball sits in the low 90s and while he repeats well, the command of the arsenal is merely average. Rom lacks a clear out pitch or above-average velocity, and developing either would leapfrog him over the long list of backend starters ahead of him. For now he remains more intriguing, but also further away than that cohort.

20 — Brenan Hanifee RHP
Born: 05/29/98 Age: 22 Bats: R Throws: R Height: 6'5" Weight: 215
Origin: Round 4, 2016 Draft (#121 overall)

Hanifee is your typical sinker-slider guy, relying on a steady supply of grounders to get outs and holding his breath every time he elevates a pitch anywhere near the middle. He sits around 90-92 with a two-seamer that pretty consistently shows late arm-side run and sink. This pitch is especially effective against same-side hitters and generates its share of weak rollers to the left side of the infield. His low-80s slider is above-average, and he often uses it to sneak strikes on lefties via the backdoor. Sometimes short and tight and sometimes slurvier, he'll also use it for a swing-and-miss from a righty every now and then. The changeup is his third pitch at the moment, but if he can improve it it would be a very useful weapon against lefties. He by and large improved as the season went on but 2019 was a step back overall, and while the command is fine the stuff really isn't overwhelming. Next he'll either look to conquer Advanced-A or corral Double-A on the fly.

Baltimore Orioles 2020

Personal Cheeseball

PC

Mason McCoy   IF
Born: 03/31/95   Age: 25   Bats: R   Throws: R   Height: 6'0"   Weight: 175
Origin: Round 6, 2017 Draft (#188 overall)

On these pages, there will be sidearming relievers, lefties with a change, Wilson's favorite beefy sluggers, and grind-em-out utility infielders. Mason McCoy is the last of those types, and the answer to the question, "What if Cadyn Grenier weren't good enough defensively to go in the first round of the draft?" Perhaps that's a bit harsh on McCoy, who was a priority senior sign who has had to prove it at every level of the minors. So far, so good, as he's hit enough, and held down both middle infield spots to make it to Double-A. There's not much in the way of power projection here, and he's merely passable at shortstop, but McCoy grinds out at-bats and makes enough good contact that his level-by-level progress could very well keep going until he finds himself with a major league bench spot.

Low Minors Sleeper

LMS

Toby Welk   3B/1B
Born: 05/02/97   Age: 23   Bats: R   Throws: R   Height: 6'2"   Weight: 205
Origin: Round 21, 2019 Draft (#618 overall)

Welk is the first player drafted from the rather prolix school of Penn State Berks, a college of Pennsylvania State University. He's more athletic than the "21st round Div. III corner infield senior sign" biography would suggest. There's feel for contact too, but Welk is going to have to hit at every level from here to Bowie just to even end up in Mason McCoy territory. But given that the author first came to fame on the prospect internet for suggesting Josh Satin had a major-league future, Welk will at worst remain a personal cheeseball for years to come.

Top Talents 25 and Under (as of 4/1/2020)

1. Adley Rutschman
2. Grayson Rodriguez
3. Ryan Mountcastle
4. DL Hall
5. Ryan McKenna
6. Yusniel Díaz
7. Anthony Santander
8. Renato Núñez
9. Chance Sisco

10. Adam Hall

The top four names on the prospect list are the slam-dunk top four under-25 talents in the organization as well. I'll leave it up to the reader to decide whether that's due in greater part to the star potential at the top of the system (which is real) or the dearth of foundational talent currently at the big league level. Adley Rutschman was the clearest-cut first overall pick in several years, and Grayson Rodriguez, Ryan Mountcastle, and DL Hall should all eventually end up high-level big leaguers in some form. Rutschman of course looks like an excellent two-way catcher, while Rodriguez and Hall look like mid-rotation arms or more, and high-leverage relievers even if some things go awry. Mountcastle has never really had a position but the bat's always played and there's an opening in Baltimore at the cold corner.

Ryan McKenna and Yusniel Díaz show enough upside that even given the risks in their profiles they deserve to slot in ahead of outfielder Anthony Santander and corner-infielder Renato Núñez, who emerged amid the rubble of the 2019 Orioles as solid contributors, but are likely not a lot more than that. Chance Sisco was nearer to the top of this list a few years ago, but he's never truly managed to assuage concerns about his work behind the plate. He split time between Baltimore and Triple-A Norfolk last season, and his bat suffered when he was with the big club. Adam Hall isn't dripping with upside like some of the names higher up on the list, but he's a decent middle-infielder who can hit more than a little and seems a safe bet to be a part of conversation in the coming years.

Part 3: Featured Articles

The Baseball Is Juiced (Again)

Robert Arthur

This article originally appeared at Baseball Prospectus on April 5, 2019.

It started when the normally reliable Chris Sale got lit up for three homers by the Mariners in the Red Sox's season opener. It was part of a record number of taters that flew on Opening Day, as starters from Sale to Zack Greinke were taken deep by the handful. Then Christian Yelich hit a home run in each of his first four games, tying yet another MLB record, this one for consecutive games with a dinger to start a season.

It didn't take long for fans and players to begin whispering and tweeting about the baseballs being juiced again. It's early yet for us to come to any definitive conclusion about the 2019 season, but preliminary data shows that the baseball has returned to its aerodynamic peak. Whether that means this season will smash home run records like 2017 did remains to be seen.

Before home run explosion over the last few years, no one worried too much about the baseball's air resistance. While MLB and Rawlings (the company that manufactures the official baseballs) kept track of dozens of metrics to make sure that the ball was consistent from month to month, they didn't measure drag.

But drag is incredibly important in determining how likely a hitter is to knock one out of the park. As baseballs become more aerodynamic, they travel further given a certain initial velocity. A deep fly ball that might have been caught at the warning track can instead go into the first row of the stands. A three percent change in drag coefficient can work to add about five feet to a well-hit fly ball, which can in turn increase home runs league wide by an astounding 10-15 percent.

It's possible to measure the aerodynamics of the baseball using the pitch-tracking radars currently in place in each MLB ballpark. By calculating the loss of speed from when the pitch is released to when it crosses the plate, you can directly measure the drag coefficient on the baseball. I first wrote about the role of decreasing drag in boosting home runs in 2017, and MLB's commission of scientists and statisticians later confirmed that the more aerodynamic baseballs in use that year were largely to blame for the spike in home runs. The same commission rejected some alternate hypotheses, like rising temperatures and a league-wide boost in launch angle pushing more balls over the fence.

The current era has featured some large fluctuations in drag coefficient, leading to first an explosion in 2016 and 2017, and then a dialing back of homers last year. Curious about the record-breaking home run tallies in the last few days, I used the same methodology to measure the aerodynamics of the baseballs so far in 2019.

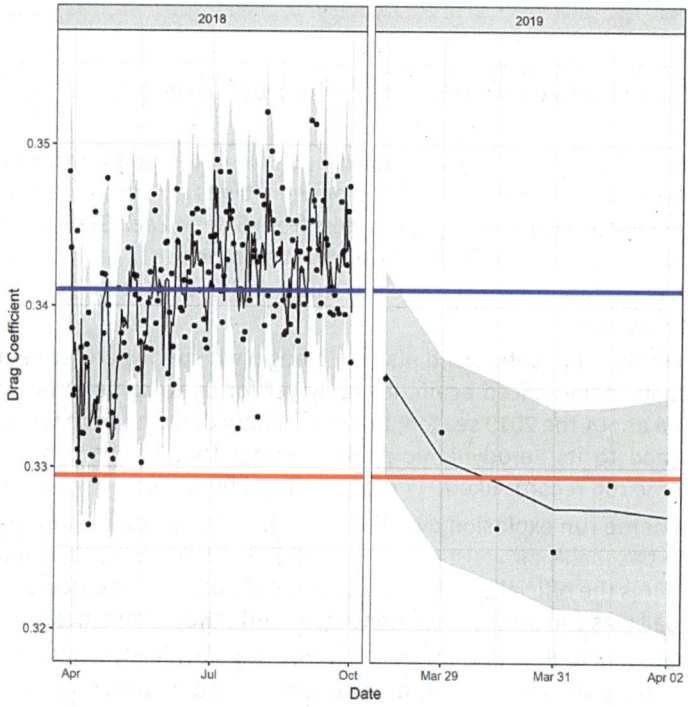

We're only a week into the 2019 season, but the drag numbers so far are among the lowest recorded in the last calendar year. With apologies for gory math, the current 2019 season average drag coefficient (the red line) would be below the 95 percent credible interval (the shaded area) for about nine-tenths of the 2018 season. (I used a Bayesian Random Walk model implemented in INLA to calculate these credible intervals, averaging the drag numbers in each game and adjusting for park.)

There were only a handful of six-day stretches in 2018 that had drag numbers below what we're seeing now, and most were in late June and early July. All of this means that 2019's data so far is quite a bit different than what we saw through most of last year.

These drag coefficients factor out the effects of temperature and air density, so they aren't a product of April cold. However, the numbers could be deceptive if the radars used to track pitches have changed from year to year. I consulted with some experts within baseball who were not aware of any specific modifications to the radar this year that could produce this pattern, but it's an important caveat of which to be aware.

On the one hand, it's only been six days, and we don't quite have the statistical basis to say that these drag coefficients are unprecedented compared to 2018. On the other hand, we've witnessed about 5,000 fastballs so far this season, so it's not as if our sample size is small. At least so far, the baseball has played like it's much more aerodynamic than it was last year. In fact, the current drag coefficient is really only comparable to 2017, when the baseballs were more aerodynamic than they had been in at least a decade.

It's not just fancy radar tracking indicating that the baseball is flying through the air more easily. The current number of home runs per game (as of this writing) is the highest it's been since the heady days of 2017, the year that teams and players broke dinger-related records everywhere you looked. That's especially remarkable considering that we're in what is typically the coldest part of the regular season, when lower temperatures and higher winds tend to suppress offense and keep balls in the air within the park. Comparing only from April to April, this year's rate of home runs per fly ball is even a little bit higher than it was in 2017.

With that said, the current measurements are no guarantee that 2019 will be another year of record-shattering homer hitting. The trouble with the drag measurements is that they are not consistent from June to August, from week to week, or even sometimes from day to day. Whether because of natural manufacturing variation or differences in the underlying supplies of cowhide and thread that go into the baseballs, drag has a tendency to fluctuate up and down over the course of a year. So the homers that fly in the first week of April wouldn't necessarily clear the fence a week later.

It's possible that this one-week drop in drag coefficient subsides and the baseball returns to its 2018 levels. On the other hand, it's almost equally probable that the ball becomes even more slippery and flies ever farther. Either way, it's clear that the baseball's air resistance is something to keep an eye on for the remainder of the 2019 season.

—*Robert Arthur is an author of Baseball Prospectus.*

The Moral Hazard of Playing It Safe

Craig Goldstein

This article originally appeared at Baseball Prospectus on August 6, 2019.

A couple days prior to the trade deadline, amidst a sea of tranquility posing as the lead up to the trade deadline, Bob Nightengale took to Twitter. Nightengale, who was probably wearing his pants backwards at the time, tweeted that MLB GMs were coming around on the idea that the unified trade deadline should be moved back from July 31 to August 15, so they could better assess their positions in the standings and whether they should buy or sell. To which I said:

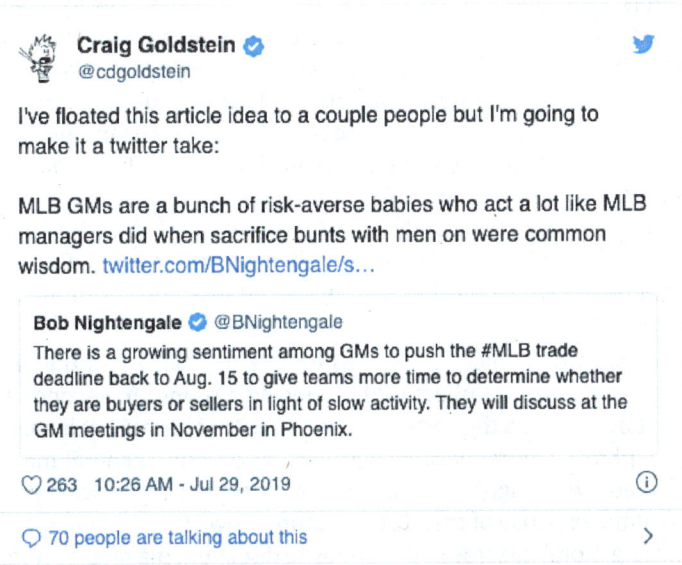

This might strike some as reductive and churlish. And it might be that, but it isn't really wrong, either. Jeff Quinton wrote a great piece discussing the environmental factors that enable front offices to avoid risk without upsetting the apple cart within their own fanbases. I don't believe that it goes far enough, however. His article gives us the proper framework through which to understand why these behaviors have been allowed to seep into front offices throughout the league. Understanding the reasons behind these actions are different from excusing them, though, and GMs should not be let off the hook for their non-competitive approach to the trade deadline (much less the offseason).

⚾   ⚾   ⚾

It's fair to say that fans as a group have rarely, if ever, been pro-player. It is also fair to say that in the time during and following the Moneyball revolution, the pendulum swung from fans who cared intensely about winning in the moment (and thus might be intolerant of a rebuilding approach) to fans who supported building a team that could compete throughout multiple seasons, viewing the playoffs as a crapshoot, with the thought that getting multiple bites at the apple was a better approach than taking a bigger bite in any one season.

There's nothing wrong with that approach, and I still find merit in that argument. However, it seems that the pendulum has swung too far in that direction. Teams are overvaluing some of the individual factors that make themselves long-term contenders rather than attempting to seize a championship when given the opportunity. It's a difficult needle to thread.

And surely, they (and those in similar positions) would have liked another two weeks to clarify where they stand so as to better marshal their resources. We've all asked for a few more minutes when staring at a menu. But all of these GMs and front office personnel are where they are to make difficult decisions. They have proprietary data and internal analysts dedicated to understanding their position relative to the rest of the league, and how any move in the here and now impacts their long-term vision. To complain (if that report is accurate) that over half the season is not enough to properly assess their season is bullshit of the highest order. Move the deadline, and you'd simply have increasingly discounted trade offers because teams would be acquiring even less control of anyone they're acquiring, rental or not.

Major league front offices are behaving like the managers they lampooned two decades ago. They're effectively sacrificing a runner to second in the ninth inning—not because it's the correct move, but rather because it is safe. It used to be that the phrase "moral hazard" was used to describe general managers who made ill-fated, short-sighted decisions aimed at locking in wins and securing their jobs at the expense of their team's future. Now, general managers are guilty of committing moral hazards in the opposite direction, playing it utterly safe and terrified of becoming scapegoats.

In lieu of bold action, they opt to pussyfoot around a current window of contention, choosing instead to play the long game and stack up years of control like they're blocks in a game of Jenga. GMs pass on signing quality players in free agency because the back-end of the deal might look bad, and because they might be able to squeeze out 70 percent of the production from a player who costs a tenth as much. That's a safer investment, too, because it's also hard to prove a negative—it's impossible to prove that Manny Machado would make the Mets a playoff team in 2019-2020, but it's easy to say that the back half of Robinson Cano's contract sucks. Owners, who rule over GM's jobs, are also humans with human brain processes that will always make the so-called albatross contract uglier than the road not taken.

These days, GMs are remembered for the bad deals they make and the surplus value they generate, not the acquisition of expensive, necessary talents that meet their market worth (or fall slightly short while still providing significant on-field value). And front offices know that one or two expensive misfires can cost them their jobs, no matter how many good deals they make.

No front office exemplifies this ethos more than the Toronto Blue Jays. General Manager Ross Atkins had this to say following the Blue Jays underwhelming trade deadline:

This is by no means the first time that an executive will cite years of control to justify their actions, which is often just another way of saying "don't look at what we got, look at how much we got of it." Atkins touts quantity to elide the discussion of quality—either, that of the players acquired, or those given up. Remember: the other teams presumably value years of control, too.

Atkins also had some thoughts to offer regarding free agents back in early 2018:

This ignores, of course, whether the player can create enough value in the front end of a contract to justify the longer term of a deal, and the decline that often occurs in the back end. It also ignores whether the player can fill a need the team requires and put them in a position to compete for and win a championship. But as teams seemingly avoid contention at all, where they might end up having to consider and later justify some of these tough decisions, we still see risk-averse approaches.

Anthony Fenech's article on two trades that recently extended GM Al Avila didn't make got at this issue rather well:

> Passing on those deals was defensible: Both players had yet to break out and trading [Michael] Fulmer—a pitcher who appeared to be a future ace, no matter his injury concerns—would have taken serious gumption, opening Avila up to strong criticism.

Avoiding strong criticism is something each of us can understand as a motivation, but the avoidance of criticism only matters if that criticism is valid. In Fulmer's case, shoving his injury concerns aside affects not only the years that the team controls him (he is currently missing a full season due to Tommy John surgery) but also the quality of those seasons, as his knee and elbow injuries combined to dampen his effectiveness even when healthy enough to pitch. But it was easy to present the then-current image of Fulmer as a top of the rotation pitcher who the team had under its domain for the next five seasons as something to build around. The status quo isn't nearly as often second-guessed as a decision that disrupts it.

⚾ ⚾ ⚾

MLB GMs are risk-averse to a fault. They are ivy-educated and consulting firm-approved, and yet they can't seem to avoid leaving wins on the table in their all-consuming lust for a non-existent $/WAR championship. They are supposed to zig when everyone else zags, and not merely pay lip service to the idea of zigging through a calculated PR plan built on convincing the fan base their approach is novel when it actually apes most of their competitors. Instead they've become far more concerned with making safe, accepted-by-the-new-common-wisdom decisions, such that our prior understanding of what a moral hazard is has become inverted.

I can't blame them entirely, and not only because of the reasons that Quinton illuminated in his article, but also because of the damage wrought by the introduction of the second wild card (WC2) spot. MLB's desire to have more teams in playoff contention has sparked anti-competitive behavior. Teams know now that they do not need to swing big as they assemble their roster because there is a good chance that a mediocre team can either catch fire and capture a division, or muddle along until they back into the WC2.

Simultaneously, the one-game playoff has neutered the WC1, putting an entire season on the flip of a coin like some sort of baseball-obsessed Anton Chigurh. While the one-game playoff makes sense as a way to increase the value of winning a division, it also means that if a front office doesn't like its chances of overcoming a behemoth like the Dodgers or Astros in the offseason, they have few incentives to chase glory. Similarly, the relative inaction in the NL Central at the trade deadline—despite a wide open division—can be explained by the idea that any high-variance investment could still result in only a wild card (or worse) result, given the mere two months left in the season to make an impact.

⚾ ⚾ ⚾

As stated at the top, we should not confuse reasons for excuses. The implementation of the second wild card is just one of many environmental factors that influence how each front office operates. I am convinced that it is one of the larger factors, but I am also convinced that organizations need to shed the yoke of "efficiency at all costs" so that they can instead pursue competition, as the spirit of the game intends. Until they do, we're all deadline losers.

—*Craig Goldstein is an author of Baseball Prospectus.*

Index of Names

Akin, Keegan 107, 125
Alberto, Hanser 20
Armstrong, Shawn 60
Bailey, Brandon 114
Bannon, Rylan 112, 126
Baumann, Michael 114, 123
Blach, Ty 62
Bleier, Richard 64
Brooks, Aaron 66
Castro, Miguel 68
Cobb, Alex 70
Davis, Chris 22
Davis, Taylor 101
Diaz, Yusniel 112, 121
Diplan, Marcos 114
Eades, Ryan 114
Eshelman, Tom 114
Fry, Paul 72
Givens, Mychal 74
Grenier, Cadyn 102, 123
Hall, Adam 112, 121
Hall, DL 108, 119
Hanhold, Eric 114
Hanifee, Brenan 127
Harvey, Hunter 76, 126
Hays, Austin 24, 124
Henderson, Gunnar 112, 124
Hess, David 78
Holaday, Bryan 26
Iglesias, José 28
Karns, Nate 109
Kline, Branden 80
Kremer, Dean 114, 122
LeBlanc, Wade 82
Lowther, Zac 114, 125
Mancini, Trey 30
Martin, Richie 32
McCoy, Mason 128
McKenna, Ryan 103, 120
Means, John 84
Milone, Tommy 87
Mountcastle, Ryan 104, 118
Mullins, Cedric 34
Núñez, Renato 36
Ortiz, Luis 110
Phillips, Evan 89
Rodriguez, Grayson 111, 118
Rogers, Josh 114
Rom, Drew 127
Rondón, José 38
Ruiz, Rio 40
Rutschman, Adley 105, 117
Santander, Anthony 42
Scott, Tanner 91
Scott, Tayler 93
Sedlock, Cody 114
Severino, Pedro 44
Shepherd, Chandler 114
Sisco, Chance 46
Smith Jr, Dwight 106
Stewart, DJ 48
Stewart, Kohl 114

Baltimore Orioles 2020

Stowers, Kyle 112
Sucre, Jesús 50
Sulser, Cole 114
Tate, Dillon 95
Trumbo, Mark 52
Ureña, Richard 54
Valaika, Pat 56
Welk, Toby 128
Wells, Alex 112, 125
Wilkerson, Stevie 58
Williams, Mason 112
Wojciechowski, Asher 97
Wynns, Austin 112
Ynoa, Gabriel 99
Zimmermann, Bruce 114, 127